NGOs and Civil Society

For my husband, Robin Mearns and my family, who have increased my capacity enormously.

NGOs and Civil Society

Democracy by Proxy?

Ann C. Hudock

Polity Press

First published in 1999 by Polity Press in association with Blackwell Publishers Ltd

Reprinted 2001

Editorial office:
Polity Press
65 Bridge Street
Cambridge CB2 1UR, UK

Marketing and production:
Blackwell Publishers Ltd
108 Cowley Road
Oxford OX4 1JF, UK

Published in the USA by
Blackwell Publishers Inc.
350 Main Street
Malden, MA 02148, USA

A catalogue record for this book is available from the British Library.

Library of Congress Cataloging-in-publication Data

Hudock, Ann.
    NGOs and civil society : democracy by proxy? / Ann C. Hudock.
        p. cm.
    Includes bibliographical references (p.) and index.
    ISBN 0-7456-1648-8 (alk. paper) -- ISBN 0-7456-1649-6 (pbk. : alk. paper)
    1. Non-governmental organizations. 2. Civil society. 3. Democracy. I. Title.

HD60 .H83 1999
060--dc21

99-037855

Typeset in 10½ on 12½ pt Palatino
by York House Typographic Ltd, London
Printed in Great Britain by T.J. International, Padstow, Cornwall

This book is printed on acid-free paper.

Contents

Acknowledgements

I would like to thank the University of Dayton, particularly the President, Bro. Raymond Fitz, S.M., Bro. Stanley Mathews, S.M., and Bro. Phil Aaron, S.M., whose financial support made possible the year I spent in Sierra Leone, and whose friendship continues to inspire me. To ARD, its staff, and their families, this book would not have been written if you had not allowed me to volunteer as a projects assistant with you from 1990 to 1991. That experience changed my life. Thank you. Special thanks are due to all the NGOs that agreed to participate in this DPhil research, and to the Rotary International Foundation for providing the International Ambassadorial Scholarship that made the first year of it possible.

Mark Robinson, my DPhil supervisor at the Institute of Development Studies, was instrumental in shaping earlier drafts of this material. John Clark at the World Bank gave me very substantive and helpful comments on the World Bank chapter. The Center for Democracy and Governance at the United States Agency for International Development afforded me the opportunity to work as a Democracy Fellow from 1997 to 1998, when I finalized this manuscript in between other responsibilities. Finally, a personal debt of gratitude is owed to Mrs Cavanaugh as well as the Newcomb family. They know why.

Glossary

ADF	African Development Foundation
APSO	Irish Agency for Personal Service Overseas
ARD	Association for Rural Development
BINGO	Benin Indigenous NGO Strengthening
BRAC	Bangladesh Rural Advancement Committee
CAF	Charities Aid Foundation
CARE	Cooperative for Assistance and Relief Everywhere
CCSL	Council of Churches Sierra Leone
CMC	Community Management Committees
CONGO	Conference of Non-Governmental Organizations
CRS	Catholic Relief Services
ECOSOC	Economic and Social Council
FLO	foundation-like organization
GAFNA	Gambia Food and Nutrition Association
GARDA	Gambia Rural Development Agency
HNISP	Health and Nutrition Institutional Support Progam
IDA	International Development Assistance
IDDI	Instituto Dominicano de Desarrollo Integral
KAP	Kamaworni Agricultural Project
LRD	Lower River Division
MCIC	Macedonia Center for International Cooperation
MLA	multilateral assistance agency
NBD	North Bank Division
NGO	non-governmental organization
NPI	New Partnerships Intitiative

ODA	overseas development assistance
OECD	Organization for Economic Co-operation and Development
OREINT	Organization for Research and Extension of Intermediate Technology
PDVSA	Petroleos de Venezuela
PRITECH	Primary Health Care Technologies
SCF/USA	Save the Children Fund/USA
SEWA	Self Employed Women's Association
SIDA	Swedish International Development Agency
UNDP	United Nations Development Programme
USAID	United States Agency for International Development
WARF	West Africa Rural Foundation
WHO	World Health Organization

1 Non-Governmental Organizations: Pawns or Practitioners?

This is a book about non-governmental organizations (NGOs), those organizations outside the realm of government, and distinct from the business community. Often referred to as the 'third sector', NGOs are characterized by their non-profit status and, in some cases, a value-based orientation or a cadre of volunteers carrying out the organizations' mandates. This book does not explore the whole realm of NGOs, but rather focuses on a subset of the sector: those NGOs working in the field of international development. Well-known examples include Catholic Relief Services, Oxfam, Bread for the World, Save the Children, and Christian Aid.

The origins of this book can be traced to a year I spent in Sierra Leone volunteering as a projects assistant for an indigenous NGO called the Association for Rural Development (ARD). During that year, I saw many of ARD's community development endeavours thwarted by (mostly) well-meaning donors and other NGOs which wanted to support ARD's work with farmers but which were unwilling or unable to give up control of critical decisions regarding what resources they would give, where and how they could be used, and whether or not they had been used well.

As a 'southern NGO', the term used to refer to those NGOs located in less-developed countries, whether in the southern hemisphere or not, ARD was beholden to those organizations which provided its resources. The irony was that these donors, or 'northern NGOs', as those organizations located in more developed countries are called, supported ARD because they believed that it was well placed to assist communities, given that ARD staff spoke local languages, knew local communities, and were aware of the political context in which development activities took place. Yet the ways in which the northern NGOs channelled resources to ARD undermined rather than enhanced ARD's capacity and ability to work with community groups.

The argument developed in this book is quite simple, yet it is enormously important if NGOs are to realize their potential for contributing to the development process by helping to alleviate poverty and to empower the poor. The thesis is this: the way in which financial resources are channelled to NGOs, and the nature of relationships forged in the process, determine NGOs' capacity. Currently, the way most NGOs seek and receive resources from their external environments subjects them to external control and leaves them unable to contribute to the process of civil society development by empowering people to voice their own needs and to make claims on government to meet those needs. Analysis of NGOs' capacity has long overlooked external factors such as these in favour of internal factors such as leadership and organizational structure. Discussions have focused on how NGOs use resources, rather than on how they acquire them and the implications this process has for their autonomy and, therefore, credibility.

NGO Financing

NGOs' development work is supported through a number of sources, and most NGOs receive a combination of any of the following: contracts; donations; grants; fees for services rendered; product sales; membership fees. An NGO's funding source will in part determine the degree of autonomy it has in developing programmes and in working with target groups. For example, some NGOs receive all of their funds from donors to carry out donors' programmes with the groups to which the donors have assigned highest priority. In these cases, the NGOs are essentially contractors and are little more than extensions of the donor agencies. When NGOs receive government funds they must follow stringent accounting and reporting requirements, which can constrain their ability to act flexibly and responsively. At the other end of the scale are organizations which receive assistance through donations solicited from the public. NGOs can use this money however they see fit and there are few if any lines of accountability to the individual donor.

Increasingly, bilateral assistance has been channelled to NGOs, especially those in developing countries. The Organization for Economic Cooperation and Development (OECD) reports that the proportion of total aid from member countries channelled through NGOs rose from 0.7 per cent in 1975 to 3.6 per cent in 1985, and at least 5 per cent in 1993/94, some US$2.3 billion in absolute terms. Snapshots of individual donors' assistance to NGOs reveal the dramatic increase in the pace as well as levels of funding awarded. The UK-based Overseas Development Institute reports that in the 10 years to 1993/94, the UK increased its official funding of NGOs by almost 400 per cent. In 1994, Swedish NGOs received 85 per cent of their funding from official aid sources. In 1993, official development assistance (ODA) to Canadian NGOs reached 70 per cent, while US NGOs received 66 per cent of their funding from official sources.

Perhaps more significantly, southern NGOs have received increased amounts of direct assistance from official development sources. The European Union has over US$80 million which is available to southern NGOs. Not surprisingly, the larger, more established NGOs, such as those in Bangladesh for example, receive a disproportionate amount of the funding available for southern NGOs. In 1991–3, US$4 million was dispersed by the Swedish International Development Agency (SIDA) to Bangladeshi NGOs (Bennett and Gibbs, 1996).

With the acquisition of these resources comes a significant amount of political clout. Evidence of southern NGOs' prominence is mounting, even if this is predominantly limited to a core of elite NGOs with connections to northern NGOs and donors. As a result of these southern NGOs' efforts, the development rhetoric is changing, even if the reality lags behind. Some southern NGOs are lobbying their own governments to respond to people's needs, challenging multilateral organizations like the World Bank to operate more transparently and accountably, and demanding that northern NGOs divest responsibilities and resources that they have traditionally claimed in the name of Third World development.

Central Questions and Structure

But such increased financing and political leverage are not without their price. Many southern NGOs find that as they accept government money their legitimacy as non-governmental actors is eroded and their relationships with clients at the field level are compromised. Or they may find that the administrative requirements attached to these tranches of funding are overwhelming and that the bulk of their time is spent accounting for money and reporting on how it is used, rather than working with the beneficiaries for whom the assistance was intended.

In the light of these trends in NGO financing and their effect on southern NGOs' capacity, this book has three primary tasks:

1   to provide a conceptual framework for understanding NGOs' relationships and the degree to which their interdependence with other organizations subjects southern NGOs in particular to external control;
2   to explore in depth the political nature of NGOs, often amplified when they accept money from government or foreign sources, as well as NGOs' position within the political landscape, a position which is often altered by the nature of their funding relationships;
3   to suggest how various NGOs' strategies for achieving financial sustainability have helped them to counter their dependence on others, avoid external control, and enable them to contribute more effectively to civil society development.

Subsequent chapters accomplish these goals in the following way. Chapter 2 opens with definitions of the various categories of NGO relevant to international development in order to clarify some often ambiguous terms. Discussion then turns to the inadequacies and inequalities inherent in the nature of relationships between northern and southern NGOs. The argument is made that northern NGOs have failed to support the institutional development of southern NGOs, or their work with community groups. The nature of northern NGOs' relationships with southern NGOs and the way in which northern

NGOs have channelled resources to southern NGOs have rendered southern NGOs dependent on external support. This dependence subjects southern NGOs to external control and leaves them unable to contribute to civil society development.

Chapter 3 provides a conceptual framework for analysing relationships between northern and southern NGOs and for understanding how these relationships affect southern NGOs' capacity. This chapter argues that the key determinants of southern NGOs' capacity are the number and nature of their relationships with organizations in the external environment. This framework addresses gaps in the literature by focusing on external rather than internal factors, particularly how NGOs acquire resources. The political nature of NGOs is fully revealed through analysis of the way they manoeuvre and manipulate their external environments in order to extract resources from them.

The framework is then applied in chapter 4. After capacity building has been defined, strategies and mechanisms undertaken to increase southern NGOs' capacity are reviewed, and then discussed as they relate to civil society development. For the most part, these strategies have rendered southern NGOs vulnerable to external control, and as such undermined the very capacities that northern NGOs have sought to enhance. Southern NGOs' contribution to civil society development are limited by their inability to evolve into actors which can strategically extract resources from the external environment while maintaining a relative degree of autonomy from those organizations providing the resources. As long as southern NGOs are beholden to interests other than those of the community groups they aim to serve, they are not making a meaningful contribution to civil society development.

Chapter 5 explores how multilateral organizations and donors inform and shape the work of northern NGOs by driving the policy agenda and providing the resources which underpin northern NGOs' work with southern NGOs. As multilateral organizations and donors engage with southern NGOs directly, this increasingly draws the latter into the political fray. It also complicates the politics of relationships between northern and southern NGOs, since their respective roles are no longer clear and traditional power paradigms of northern NGO dominance are being challenged. This chapter argues that if multilateral organizations' and donors' goals of civil society development are to be met through southern NGOs, then northern NGOs' support for southern NGOs will have to be altered in such a way that the number and nature of their relationships enhances, rather than hinders, southern NGOs' autonomy and contribution to civil society.

Chapter 6 illustrates these arguments by presenting case studies of southern NGOs in Sierra Leone and The Gambia, tracing their relationships with northern NGOs, and suggesting their inadequacies both for southern NGOs as sustainable and autonomous organizations, and for their ability to engage with the community groups which they were designed to serve. Southern NGOs' resource dependence and vulnerability to external control impede their responsiveness to client groups.

Chapter 7 presents policy recommendations for reconfiguring relationships between northern and southern NGOs, and provides examples of southern NGOs which have overcome their dependence on northern NGOs by adopting innovative, sustainable financing strategies. These strategies have increased NGOs' ability to contribute to development processes, as well as to the creation of vibrant civil societies. Chapter 8 concludes that unless southern NGOs' resource dependence is addressed, and northern NGOs find ways to engage differently with them, then there will be profound implications for development theory and practice.

2 The Ties that Bind: Northern NGOs' Relationships with Southern NGOs

A northern NGO once asked ARD to assess an application that it had received from a community group in Sierra Leone. This group, a local women's cooperative, had requested that the northern NGO support its palm-oil-processing activities. Since the northern NGO had its offices in Europe, it was unable to get a real sense of what the group was doing, how well it was doing it, and whether or not it was worthy of support. So, this northern NGO turned to its local partner, ARD, to give an account of the situation. ARD's knowledge of local customs, languages, and development problems meant that it was ideally placed as an organization to determine the legitimacy of this group's request.

ARD travelled outside the capital city Freetown to meet with the women in the cooperative and to see their palm-oil-processing activities. As ARD arrived, the village drum was sounded, calling villagers to a meeting where their project activities would be discussed and their request for assistance reviewed. The village hut filled up quickly as the women welcomed the opportunity to make their pitch directly to these outsiders who would help to bring assistance to this village, where infant mortality rates were high, literacy rates low, and employment opportunities scarce. The communities' needs were real.

Unfortunately, the cooperative's efforts were not. ARD discovered this very quickly by observing group dynamics and the interaction between male leaders and female members, and by asking pointed questions about the group's work and listening carefully to the answers given, all in local languages. What might have been lost on a foreign representative of a northern NGO was abundantly clear to ARD in a very short time. The men of the village were using the women's labour as a way of developing a palm-oil-processing business. The women were a good selling point to donors since 'gender' and 'women's involvement' were a top priority for a lot of them. In fact, when asked to list the most pressing needs of the village, the women cited water as their number one priority. One older woman at the back of the hut even stood up and thanked the outsiders for supporting the water project, demonstrating her complete lack of knowledge about the project proposed or the stated activities of the cooperative. ARD's ability to discern fact from fiction demonstrates why northern NGOs seek them out as development partners.

NGOs' presumed comparative advantage in delivering development services has been described as the 'articles of faith' (Tendler, 1982). These are the characteristics of NGOs which uniquely equip them to achieve development outcomes. In comparison with governments, then, NGOs are said to have a better ability to (Fowler, 1988: 8):

- reach the poor sections of the population;
- encourage and obtain beneficiaries' participation in development activities;
- focus on processes of development as well as outcomes of the interventions;
- respond to people's needs flexibly, and therefore tailor assistance appropriately;
- work with and through local institutions;
- work cost-effectively;
- innovate and identify creative solutions to difficult problems;
- undertake people-centred research;
- learn from and apply field experience to develop solutions to problems;
- reflect the needs of people affected by development problems, and work to achieve solutions based on these field realities rather than outside analysis.

In spite of southern NGOs' advantage in working with community groups, few southern NGOs have significant time or resources available to devote to these tasks. Southern NGOs' reliance on northern NGOs for resources means that when the former are in the field, it is to carry out work for the latter. Or southern NGOs find that with increasing assistance from northern NGOs, the bulk of their time is spent in the office. ARD, for example, spent a considerable amount of its time in the office, rather than in the field, writing project reports, trip reports, funding proposals, evaluations, baseline assessments, quarterly reports, and end-of-project reports for each of the different northern NGOs with which it worked. Another chunk of ARD's time was receiving and entertaining – quite often at ARD's expense – representatives of these northern NGOs when they came to visit.

At best, a Southern NGO's reliance on northern NGOs for resources means that it can interact with community groups, even if it loses control over which groups it works with, which activities it undertakes, and how it undertakes them. At worst, southern NGOs lose touch entirely with their client groups, spending all their time in the office on administrative tasks required to maintain northern NGOs' support. Either way, there is little or no time or resources allocated for southern NGOs to develop relationships with community groups of their choosing, responding to needs as the groups, not the donors, identify them.

This chapter examines the nature of relationships between northern and southern NGOs and demonstrates the ways in which they are lacking. The so-called 'partnerships' which have been developed have been inadequate, since they tend to reinforce northern NGOs' dominance and southern NGOs' dependence on them for resources. Capacity-building strategies, explored in depth in chapter 4, have been adopted as an antidote to unequal exchanges between northern and southern NGOs because these have the potential to establish a new facilitative role for northern NGOs, while increasing the ability of southern NGOs to take on an operational role. The failure of these strategies to address external factors, however, means that they have not significantly altered the balance.

Definitions of NGOs

Northern NGOs

Northern NGOs, like those which worked with ARD, originated after the First World War, and had an even greater prominence after the Second World War. These NGOs, which included Catholic Relief Services (CRS), Oxfam, and Cooperative for Assistance and Relief Everywhere (CARE), focused primarily on delivering private contributions of relief assistance in war-torn Europe. Once the conflicts had ended and communities were gradually rebuilt, many northern NGOs shifted their geographic focus and began addressing the development problems confronting the Third World. At the same time, some extended their relief operations to include welfare and development activities (Clark, 1991: 29–31). Some worked with existing organizations like membership organizations (discussed below), whereas others delivered services directly.

Recent years have witnessed a further evolution of northern NGOs' agendas as many organizations have opted to facilitate the work of their southern counterparts rather than engage directly in development activities. This is commonly referred to as capacity building, defined here as 'an explicit outside intervention to improve an organization's performance in relation to its mission, context, resources, and sustainability, achieved through a process-oriented approach of assisting the organization to acknowledge, assess, and address its external environment'. Some northern NGOs, however, have been reluctant to cease or modify their operational work, given the financial resources that hang in the balance.

In Bosnia in 1998, for example, there were nearly 200 NGOs from 24 countries, and in that year alone it was projected that they would spend US$1 billion on activities. An article in the *New York Times* reported that there had never been such a large group of voluntary organizations with such broad responsibilities assembled in one country. While their assistance may have been appreciated by many, some analysts, according to the article, viewed these groups as 'an occupation force of foreigners who are smothering the incentive of Bosnians to take over the reconstruction of their country' (Becker, 1998: 7).

Southern NGOs

Southern NGOs, for their part, emerged partly in response to funding opportunities from northern NGOs. Some southern NGOs evolved from membership organizations, and others are outgrowths of their northern counterparts. Drawing on the Bosnia example again, foreign NGOs there helped to create 177 local NGOs which were to take over the basic tasks at first being done by foreigners in areas as varied as: medical, social, and commercial rehabilitation; loans for start-up businesses; counselling for widows and veterans; reopening of schools and job training; and establishment of human rights and democratic organizations.

Other southern NGOs, however, have formed on their own initiative, rather than donors', in response to the plethora of development problems confronting their countries. These NGOs often claim that they are driven by the desire to identify local solutions to development problems rather than accept solutions imposed from outside. Generally, southern NGOs are as varied as the problems which gave birth to them, but often these organizations resemble their northern counterparts in structure and operations, since many were initiated by former employees of northern NGOs, or received considerable financial and technical support from these organizations.

The Macedonian Center for International Cooperation (MCIC) was founded in 1993 in response to the worsening economic conditions in Macedonia stemming in part from the transition to an independent state in 1991. MCIC's goals are to promote peace, build a civic society, and assist marginalized groups. One example of how it supports the short-term needs of its target groups is its Village Water Supply Programme. This effort provides water in 38 villages with 23,883 people living in them, 9.11 per cent of whom belong to ethnic minorities, groups which are disproportionately affected by economic hardship. In order to address these communities' long-term needs, MCIC provided training in how to manage water-supply systems. Activities like these were funded by outside donors and northern NGOs, primarily the Dutch.

The Bangladesh Rural Advancement Committee (BRAC) is one of the largest southern NGOs, and perhaps the best known. It has successfully scaled up its grassroots activities so that it now employs over 4,500 people and has an annual operational budget of about US$23 million. The strategies it has employed vary, but the result has been an NGO which has made the transition from providing relief and community development assistance at the local level starting in 1972, to an NGO which currently has multi-sectoral activities, support programmes, and training and research capacity.

Intermediary NGOs

Southern NGOs often serve as what are called intermediary NGOs, meaning that their role is to support other NGOs or community groups in their work, with varying degrees of direct involvement in social service provision through, for example, agriculture, health, education, or water projects. Intermediary NGOs can be northern or southern. While some administer development projects at the field level, many help community organizations to run their own projects by providing them with training, small grants, or technical advice in areas such as proposal writing, fundraising, and project design and evaluation.

Intermediary NGOs are increasingly important to the NGO sector, particularly in developing countries, since donors and northern NGOs use them as conduits for channelling funding to other NGOs or membership organizations. In addition, in newly emerging democracies, particularly in Eastern Europe and the newly independent states, intermediaries are integral to the establishment and consolidation of the NGO sector, since truly non-governmental organizations are a new phenomenon, and the requisite skills and resources need to be developed if NGOs are to play a significant role. Intermediary NGOs help to develop these skills and to obtain international and domestic resources. Grassroots groups or membership organizations often rely on this assistance to carry out their activities or even survive.

Intermediary NGOs are not, however, a panacea. As INTRAC, the NGO training and research centre in Oxford, points out (Bennett and Gibbs, 1996: 4):

> After initial enthusiasm for supporting local NGOs as inter-
> mediaries to empower the popular organisations of Civil

Society, questions are now being asked about their account-ability to these organisations. Might they even weaken Civil Society? Have we witnessed a disproportionate support for local NGOs at the expense of popular organisations ... making the latter dependent on local NGOs as intermediaries for access to resources? Local NGOs increasingly tend to represent pop-ular organisations in policy discussions with donors and, in turn, have attracted a professional middle-class cadre of 'experts'. By funding and promoting local NGOs, are we in danger not only of encouraging opportunism but also of under-mining even the more productive role that governments might play in developing countries?

It is when southern NGOs usurp the role of their beneficiaries in the development process that they jeopardize civil society development rather than contribute to it. And when northern NGOs support intermediary organizations to the exclusion of their beneficiaries or build the former's capacity dispropor-tionately to that of the latter, they encourage democracy by proxy rather than true democracy.

Membership Organizations

The fourth and final category of organization discussed here is the community groups or membership organizations. These are local organizations formed in response to a particular development problem and working together to identify a solution. Sometimes these groups disband once the problem is solved; at other times, they identify another common com-munity concern and devote their time and energy to addressing it. Whether community-based organizations have five or 500 members, their important characteristic is their desire to engage in self-help activities. They are managed by members on behalf of members. Quite often community-based organizations are founded by charismatic leaders and their activities may not entirely reflect community concerns, but at least notionally that is their purpose. Many community-based organizations will have an elected leadership, including a treasurer, a secretary, and a president along with other more specialized positions like membership coordinator. Sometimes members are required to pay a fee for the privilege of belong-ing to the organization, or they may be obligated to contribute their labour to a collective project. Community organizations, at least in theory, combine individual benefits with collective gains.

An example of a membership organization is the Self Employed Women's Association (SEWA) of Ahmedabad, India (Clark, 1991: 95). SEWA, established in 1972 as a trade union of women in the informal sector, was created in response to the high interest rates charged by moneylenders which threatened the profitability of women's micro-enterprise endeavours. By establishing its own bank, which provided loans at 12 per cent interest, SEWA has been able to finance its 13,000 members and to help them increase their daily incomes as a result.

After several decades of northern NGOs, southern NGOs, and community groups working separately and together to address development problems, concerns surfaced regarding the respective roles and responsibilities of each type of organization. Throughout the 1970s and 1980s, debate focused on who should take the lead in development: the north with its surfeit of resources and technology, or the south with its vested interest in solving development problems and its indigenous knowledge of how to solve them? Northern NGOs were accused of dominating the development process, southern NGOs began clamouring for more space and support in order to carry out their own development agendas, and community groups were often overlooked, since they tended to obtain their development resources through an intermediary, whether northern or southern, and as a result had little say as to the nature of that assistance. Decisions rested with the northern and southern NGOs.

Politics of NGO Relationships

Tensions between northern and southern NGOs over their respective roles led to the May 1998 launch in Brussels of the International Forum on Capacity Building. The multi-stakeholder Forum is a mechanism to inform relationships and to foster dialogue between northern and southern NGOs, donors, and foundations. It is designed to help shape conceptual approaches, policies and practices for future capacity-building interventions. Regional consultations in Africa, Asia, and Latin America, and a survey of northern NGO and donor approaches to capacity building, revealed that the stakeholders had different priorities for capacity building, and that the NGOs in each region differed in their ordering of needs. The common themes that arose, which will be used to structure the work of the Forum over the next several years, were the need for:

- leadership development;
- policy research and advocacy;
- information access, use and dissemination;
- building alliances, coalitions, networks, North–South partnerships, and inter-sectoral partnerships;
- financial sustainability.

Southern NGOs are demanding more resources and more responsibility in deciding on the allocation of resources. Southern NGOs charge that northern NGOs, as a result of their access to foreign currency and equipment, enjoy preferential treatment from host country governments, and northern NGOs' dominance marginalizes southern NGOs in their own countries. For their part, northern NGOs insist their role is essential, since they shield southern NGOs from the administrative burdens associated with accounting for donor resources. Northern NGOs say that they provide essential training to southern NGOs in order to help them develop their skills, which will enable them one day to lead development. Northern NGOs insist that most southern NGOs are not ready to do this, particularly because they lack the capacity to plan project activities, mobilize resources to carry them out, and account for the resources used. Both northern and southern NGOs recognize that there is a need to develop trust for one another and to foster mutual respect if their relationships are to improve.

Northern and southern NGOs often provide assistance to community groups through their collaborative efforts, so improving these relationships is essential to raising the quality of development services delivered at the field level. Northern NGOs often rely on southern NGOs to act as intermediaries, providing information about community groups and facilitating access to them. Southern NGOs rely on northern NGOs for resources which will enable them to work with community groups and to respond to their needs. Ultimately, the goal is to strengthen community groups' ability to achieve development aims by embarking on sustainable activities.

The extent to which local communities can identify and address their own needs is evidence of the existence of 'social capital', that is the degree of trust, reciprocity, and engagement between individuals in a particular society. Social capital can be produced when local actors interact with external actors, thus 'thickening' civil society (Fox, 1996: 1089). It is not entirely clear, however, that southern NGOs can contribute to social capital development, since quite often they are responding less to the community's needs than to those of the donor or northern NGOs. As Agbaje (1990: 36) pointed out in the context of southern NGOs' contribution to civil society development in Africa:

> the role of local charities and local NGOs, often times brought into being by the elite, can amount to little more than tokenism in the area of grassroots development. In fact, while local NGOs have long formed part of the drive toward grassroots development in East Africa, their recent appearance in a more visible manner along the West African coast has raised questions as to the extent to which they do form part of the coping mechanism of the local elite, in the face of pains of structural adjustment, intent on using them to attract foreign funding subsequently to disappear into private pockets.

Renshaw (1994: 47) voices the concerns of many when she says that supporting southern NGOs 'does not in and of itself strengthen civil society'. Southern NGOs contribute to civil society only when they build organizational capacity at the community level, develop replicable service delivery models, and contribute to policy debates. As Pearce (1993: 225) says:

> An authentic civil society must involve the poor and the weak gaining real and meaningful rights as citizens, genuinely enfranchised and able to build organizations to defend their interests. It is about the rights of individuals to associate voluntarily. Constructing civil society cannot be essentially about building up intermediary development organizations to represent the 'poor': it must be about empowering the poor and enabling them to fight for their own rights as citizens.

Two points are critical with respect to southern NGOs' provision of basic services to grassroots groups and the contribution this may make to civil society development. First, the process involved in the provision of goods or services is as important as, if not more important than, the end result. If southern NGOs provide assistance in a way that encourages dependency and fails to mobilize skills and resources locally, then the southern NGOs may do more harm than good in the long term. Second, the nature of southern NGOs' relationships with northern NGOs often determines how the former work with community groups, since very few northern NGOs provide resources for southern NGOs to use at their own discretion. More often, this assistance is tied to a particular project or activity of the northern NGOs' choosing.

Transforming partnerships between northern and southern NGOs will help the latter to realize their potential comparative advantage in assisting community groups by allowing them to support these groups in a way which does not encourage dependency or impose external agendas. The next chapter provides a conceptual framework for analysing degrees of interdependence between NGOs, and for understanding how this interdependence affects southern NGOs' ability to assist community groups and contribute to social capital formation and, as a result, to civil society development.

3 Analysing Institutional Interdependence: A Conceptual Framework

'Independence: That's middle-class blasphemy. We are all dependent on one another, every soul of us on earth.' So said Professor Higgins in George Bernard Shaw's *Pygmalion*. He could very well have been talking about NGOs; they all rely on other organizations for something, whether it is access to community groups, resources, or technical assistance. Many southern NGOs, for example, lack the resources they need to carry out development work with their client groups, so they seek these resources from northern NGOs. Quite often when northern NGOs provide these resources it is they, rather than the southern NGOs or community groups, that determine how these should be used. Northern NGOs' access to and control over development resources place them in a position of power relative to southern NGOs.

This chapter presents a framework for analysing NGOs' interdependence, and demonstrates how the asymmetry of these relationships has subjected southern NGOs to external control and jeopardized their ability to contribute to a strong, association-based civil society by assisting grassroots groups. After identifying gaps in the existing literature, the chapter provides the rationale for a framework of what is here termed 'inter-organizational influence', and presents both the resource-dependence perspective and interdependence as they were originally conceived in order to establish the foundation upon which the framework was built.

The following section elaborates the framework, discussing how it furthers understanding of north–south NGO relationships. In short, the framework of inter-organizational influence suggests that southern NGOs' capacity to serve grassroots community groups effectively and to avoid external control by northern NGOs is largely determined by two factors: the number and the nature of relationships with northern NGOs.

Gaps in the Existing Literature

Gaps in the existing organizational analysis and NGO literature suggest the need for a new analytical approach to understanding southern NGOs' relationships with northern NGOs.

The organizational analysis literature, where NGOs have their analytical origins and grounding, may be wholly inappropriate for understanding and explaining NGOs for several reasons:

1   Organizational analysis has focused attention on internal rather than external aspects of organizations. Performance and sustainability have largely been ascribed to the strength of organizations' structures, management, and staff (e.g. Billis and MacKeith, 1993).
2   The majority of work within organizational analysis has focused on how organizations use the resources at their disposal rather than how organizations acquire resources. Such an approach presupposes the existence of resources. This may have been an appropriate presumption for other types of organization and context which have historically been the focus of organizational analysis, such as profit-making organizations in advanced industrial societies. In these contexts resources are generally available and accessible. Analysing non-profit southern NGOs in developing nations, however, requires a different approach, since a number of resources are physically non-existent, or not obtainable given organizations' lack of capital and access to credit. In this context, it is the absence of resources, not the distribution of existing ones, that concerns organizations and that defines the environment. This must be the starting point for any analysis of southern NGOs.

3   The organizational analysis literature fails to address in a comprehensive manner the effect that relationships between organizations have on their structures and operations, and therefore on their ability to carry out their work. One explanation for this gap is that relationships are difficult to research, since they are hard to define or even to observe, vary in quality and scope, and change over time for any number of reasons.

In the NGO literature, relationships between northern and southern NGOs have been described as partnerships, yet there are weaknesses to this approach which point to the need for a new analytical framework for understanding these relationships. The term 'partnership' reflects an idealistic notion of what interactions between northern and southern NGOs should be like, rather than providing an accurate description of what they are actually like. Many exchanges between northern and southern NGOs can be characterized as isolated incidents, rather than part of a larger process, which the term 'partnership' implies. Very few are based on the types of equal exchange which are inherent to any partnership. North–South NGO relationships have been dominated by northern NGOs, since they provide the resources necessary for development work. This tends to obscure southern NGOs' contribution to northern NGOs specifically, and to the development process generally.

In fact, partnerships could actually be disadvantageous to southern NGOs and so may not be the most appropriate type of relationship for them to enter into in order to acquire necessary resources. Given the fluidity of southern NGOs' external environments, partnerships could be disadvantageous if they committed southern NGOs to relationships which did not provide the necessary resources, or which took southern NGOs away from other activities or organizations which might be more beneficial.

One of the most fundamental weaknesses of the NGO literature is its suggestion that NGOs possess a value base that drives them to act on 'altruistic' motives. This absolutely contradicts one of the key tenets of organizational analysis; namely that organizational survival is every organization's goal and that, to survive, an organization must place its own interests before those of others, especially those which are potential competitors. As the myth is propagated that NGOs are somehow organizationally unique and operating on a value base, rather than on organizational imperatives like survival, the true complexity of NGOs' situation with respect to acquiring resources is obscured.

The goal of organizational survival is met through self-serving behaviour, and this has implications for how NGOs acquire resources and the effect it has on an organization. First, the competition for scarce resources militates against the formation of networks or coalitions, which could actually be very beneficial mechanisms for obtaining funding. Second, it is often the search for resources that shifts NGOs away from any value base that they did possess.

For example, the disparity between NGOs' values and operations were laid bare when the *Chicago Tribune* conducted a year-long inquiry into four of the leading child sponsorship organizations – organizations which espouse values based on child welfare. The March 1998 report revealed that these organizations, which were raising money on behalf of children through child sponsorship programmes, were using these as a marketing ploy, and that some of the children had been dead for years while unwitting donors continued to sponsor them. Ultimately, the *Tribune*'s investigation found that child sponsorship agencies succeeded best in providing basic services such as health, education, sanitation, and agricultural programmes for communities around the world. These same organizations, however, failed to keep the basic promise which was the premise of their appeal: that they could make a positive and lasting change in the life of a sponsored child.[1] It

---

1   For years the development community, including some of the NGOs which were part of this *Chicago Tribune* investigation, have seen child sponsorship strategies as problematic and fraught with inconsistencies. There is a growing realization that NGOs cannot alter many of the systemic constraints which so negatively affect children's welfare and survival. In addition, the marketing and advertising pitches made to the public have been reviewed by many of these agencies, often as a result of criticism that these campaigns exploit children. Many NGOs continue with child sponsorship, since it is often their only way to raise money which can be used to cover their core operating costs, as well as their development programmes.

was the need for resources that drove the marketing campaigns, not the welfare of the child (Anderson, 1998).

Conceptual Framework

The framework of inter-organizational influence is developed here out of the realization that there existed no coherent framework, supported by empirical evidence, for analysing how southern NGOs acquire resources and what impact this process has on their organizational effectiveness on the one hand, and their autonomy on the other. By bringing to light the interdependence of northern and southern NGOs, the framework provides a tool for analysing the extent to which:

1   southern NGOs' reliance on northern NGOs for resources has undermined the former's ability to interact with their client groups and to carry out programmes with them in a way which reflects the clients' priorities, rather than those of the northern NGOs';

2   northern NGOs benefit from interactions with southern NGOs;

3   strengthening southern NGOs involves altering northern NGOs' organizational structures and operations, since this may enhance southern NGOs' ability to obtain resources in a way which allows them to reach client groups and to carry out their own programmes according to identified priorities.

There are two primary building blocks of the framework. The first, the resource-dependence perspective, was developed by Pfeffer and Salancik in 1978 within the organizational analysis literature. The second, Keohane and Nye's concept of interdependence, was developed in 1977 within international relations literature. Each concept is briefly introduced here.

The Resource-Dependence Perspective

The resource-dependence perspective was one of the earliest concepts in the organizational analysis literature to deal with the problem of how organizations acquire resources instead of how they use them. Although the resource-dependence perspective draws on examples of how American businesses and firms interact with the external environment, it generalizes beyond that. As Pfeffer and Salancik point out (1978: 2), 'Organizations must transact with other elements in their environment to acquire needed resources, and this is true whether we are talking about public organizations, private organizations, small or large organizations, or organizations which are bureaucratic or organic.'

The premise underlying the resource-dependence perspective is that no organization is self-contained or self-directed. All organizations must interact with others in their external environment in order to gain resources necessary for survival. Dependence on the environment is not problematic; rather, it is the undependable nature of the environment that is so. This distinction is critical to understanding this perspective. Pfeffer and Salancik (1978: 2) contend: 'Our position is that organizations survive to the extent that they are effective. Their effectiveness derives from the management of demands, particularly the demands of interest groups upon which the organizations depend for resources and support ... The key to organizational survival is the ability to acquire and maintain resources.'

We can understand an organization's behaviour only by knowing its environment and the problems it has extracting resources from that environment. How the organization responds to external constraints is critical to its survival, since constraints on organizational action influence organizational behaviour and design. The focus of this analysis is on the organization's context. Pfeffer and Salancik (1978: 3) assert: 'What happens in an organization is not only a function of the organization, its structure, its leadership, its procedures, or its goals. What happens is also a consequence of the environment and the particular contingencies and constraints deriving from that environment.'

Organizations do, however, exercise a degree of control over their relationship with the external environment. Indeed, as Pfeffer and Salancik (1978: 13) say, 'Perhaps one of the most important influences on an organization's response to its environment is the organization itself.'

There are three related levels of the organizational environment:

1 the entire system of networked individuals and organizations which are related to each other and to a focal organization through its transactions;
2 the set of individuals and organizations with which the organization directly interacts: on this level the organization can experience the environment;
3 the organization's perception and representation of the environment: its enacted environment (1978: 63).

While no organization is entirely self-sufficient, some exist in more dependable environments than others. Organizations experience uncertainty when those controlling resources are undependable, as they often are in resource-scarce environments. This uncertainty threatens an organization's effectiveness and even survival.

Organizations are torn between their desire for autonomy and their need to control uncertainty created by dependence on the environment. The result of this tension is organizational interdependence (defined more fully in the next section).

Interdependence varies with the availability of resources relative to the demand for them. Three conditions determine how dependent one organization is on another. These are:

1 *the importance of the resource sought* to the organization seeking it. This is defined by the magnitude of that resource and its criticality. Magnitude refers to the proportion of inputs and outputs accounted for by the resource, while criticality is determined by how severe the consequences would be if the resource were not available.
2 *the level of discretion* that the holder of the resource has over its allocation and use.
3 *the existence of alternative sources* for acquiring the resource, or of an appropriate substitute for it. Do those who control the resource have a monopoly?

Organizations employ the following strategies to manage their dependencies:

- adapting to or altering the constraints faced by inter-acting with the external environment;
- altering the interdependencies through mergers, diver-sification, or growth;
- negotiating their environment by interlocking director-ships or undertaking joint ventures with other organ-izations or through other associations;
- changing the legality or legitimacy of the environment by political action.

The process of adaptation involves the following (Pfeffer and Salancik, 1978: 71):

> Organizations employ a variety of strategies for bringing stabil-ity and certainty to their environments. They may restructure the organization to avoid instability or its consequences; stabil-ize exchange relationships; or restructure the set of exchange relationships to enhance stability. Each organizational action taken to reduce uncertainty or manage problematic transactions may alter the connectedness of the system, possibly altering the transaction flows to other organizations. In other words, actions taken to manage interedependence may, in the long run, increase the interdependence among environmental elements, requiring further actions to manage the new uncertainties.

Asymmetrical Interdependence

The second tier of the framework of inter-organizational influ-ence draws on the concept of interdependence as developed by Keohane and Nye (1977) in order to suggest the varying degrees to which organizations experience interdependence, and the impact this will have on their autonomy given the costs associated with the transactions.

Definitions of a few key terms provide a useful starting point to any discussion of the interdependence perspective. 'Dependence' is a state of being determined or significantly affected by external forces. 'Interdependence' is simply mutual dependence. It is important to distinguish early on between 'interconnectedness' and 'interdependence'. Where there are reciprocal, yet not necessarily symmetrical, costly effects of transactions, interdependence exists. Where interactions do

not have significantly costly effects, the exchange can be classi-
fied as one of interconnectedness. Keohane and Nye maintain
that this distinction is vital to understanding the politics of
interdependence.

Inherent in the notion of interdependence is cost. Keohane
and Nye (1989: 9–10) write, 'Our perspective implies that
interdependent relationships will always involve costs, since
interdependence restricts autonomy; but it is impossible to
specify a priori whether the benefits of a relationship will
exceed the costs. This will depend on the values of the actors as
well as on the nature of the relationship.'

A cost-benefit analysis of interdependence can be done
according to one of two perspectives, focusing on:

1   the joint gains or the joint losses to the parties
    involved;
2   the relative gains and the distributional issues arising
    from exchanges, an approach that Keohane and Nye
    favour since they feel that the first approach may
    obscure the more critical question of who gets what.

Interdependence does not imply balanced exchanges between
actors. In fact, most relationships are characterized by asymmetry. Keohane and Nye (1989: 10) write, 'It is asymmetries in
dependence that are most likely to provide sources of influence
for actors in their dealings with one another.' In other words,
asymmetrical interdependence is a source of power.[2] The less
dependent actor has control over resources and therefore the
potential to affect outcomes. But the operative word is 'potential'. Such an advantage does not guarantee that the political
resources provided will translate into control over outcomes.

While asymmetrical interdependence may appear to favour
one actor, in reality other, unforeseen factors may serve as a
source of strength to the weaker actor. For instance, it may be
that the actor which is smaller and less powerful has the
advantage in exchanges, since:

●   it may be able to act more coherently;

2 For a very useful discussion of power, particularly how weaker actors
   may assert power in relationships, see Baldwin (1989).

- it may have a deeper commitment to an issue than the stronger actor;
- it may be willing to take risks and suffer consequences to a greater degree than the stronger actor (Keohane and Nye, 1989: 18).

In order to highlight the role of power in interdependence, Keohane and Nye distinguish between two dimensions: sensitivity and vulnerability. Sensitivity interdependence refers to the degrees of responsiveness. This can be evaluated by asking how quickly changes by one actor bring about costly changes in another, and how great are the costly effects. Vulnerability, on the other hand, considers the relative availability and costliness of alternatives that actors face. In other words, what are the costs of adjusting to the alternatives?

In sum, sensitivity and vulnerability can be understood as the degree to which the absence of a resource affects an actor. If that actor can acquire the resource elsewhere, or exist without it, then it is sensitive to the one possessing the resource. However, if the actor cannot get the resource elsewhere or exist without it, then it is vulnerable to the one possessing the resource. Vulnerability implies that the cost of adjusting to the absence of the resource is felt in a substantial way for a prolonged period of time.

Elaboration of the Framework

The framework of inter-organizational influence is unique, since it draws together two distinct bodies of literature, and applies insights gained from them to a context very different from the ones in which they were developed. The framework takes from the resource-dependence perspective its focus on how external factors – such as the number and nature of relationships with other organizations – shape organizational behaviour, and considers how the uncertainty and power dynamics of those relationships can lead to external control. In this context, the starting point of analysis is how organizations acquire resources, not only how they use them. This approach reveals the degree to which organizations possessing resources can exercise influence over those seeking resources. Adding to this perspective, Keohane and Nye's distinction between sensitivity and vulnerability interdependence results in a more robust analysis of costs associated with southern NGOs' transactions with northern NGOs.

Interdependence creates problems for organizations when there are many links with organizations in the external environment, and when there are few links with such organizations. The greater the number of organizations with which a southern NGO must interact in order to obtain essential resources, the higher the transaction costs. The more dependent a southern NGO is on numerous actors in the external environment, the more that NGO must concentrate its energies and resources on managing the demands of these actors and interactions with them. This of course draws southern NGOs away from their stated agendas, and from functioning effectively and efficiently as development organizations. Furthermore, tightly linked organizational networks may be problematic because when resources are scarce and organizational capacities are stretched, any changes in resource availability are likely to alter the delicate balance. So, southern NGOs enmeshed in webs of vulnerability interdependence are unable to cope with unexpected shocks to the system.

In Sierra Leone, for example, when the rebel war increased in intensity around 1995, many northern NGOs were closing their operations or scaling down their support for southern NGOs and community development projects. Since ARD relied so heavily on northern NGOs for assistance, both for core costs like salaries and running the office and for development projects, its organizational survival was in jeopardy. The uncertainty regarding resources meant that ARD could not plan activities or guarantee to the grassroots groups with which it worked that the projects would continue.

When northern NGOs provide southern NGOs with resources, the latter are most likely to comply with any attempts to control them if the following conditions exist.[3] First, the southern NGO is aware of the demands that the northern NGO is making on it. Second, the northern NGO provides the southern NGO with resources which are critical

---

3   These are adapted from Pfeffer and Salancik, (1978: 44).

to its survival and operations, and which it cannot receive elsewhere. Third, the southern NGO does not have any leverage on the northern NGO; that is, the southern NGO does not control any of the resources which are essential to the northern NGO's survival and operations, and therefore has no ability to control any of the latter's demands.

Because southern NGOs' contribution to North–South NGO relationships has been masked by the tendency to conceive of the exchanges as one-way, from North to South, southern NGOs are often unaware of their potential influence with northern NGOs. The latter for their part have yet to appreciate the benefits they receive from their interactions with southern NGOs.

Fourth, a southern NGO is more likely to comply with a northern NGO's control attempt when the latter is monitoring the former's activities in order to ensure compliance. Finally, a southern NGO is more likely to comply with demands made by one northern NGO when these do not conflict with those made by other northern NGOs upon which the southern NGO is dependent for resources.

In reality, however, southern NGOs face conflicting and competing demands, not just from the northern NGOs but from the other stakeholders with which they work. Southern NGOs' survival depends on their ability to meet each of these groups' demands effectively by prioritizing the competing ones and appeasing conflicting interests. Southern NGOs often find that they are caught between the conflicting demands of membership organizations on the one hand and those of northern NGOs on the other. Managing each set of relationships requires very different types of response. Quite often the programmes and priorities of northern NGOs do not align with those of membership organizations, and southern NGOs find themselves in the awkward position of implementing a programme that they do not support, or that does not wholly match the needs of the communities for which it is intended.

Southern NGOs' legitimacy is derived from their work with membership organizations; therefore, they must nurture and maintain these relationships. At the same time, southern NGOs rely on northern NGOs for the resources they need to exist and to carry out their work with membership organizations. In fact, northern NGOs' resource flows to southern

NGOs are predicated on the latter's interactions with membership organizations. If southern NGOs alienate membership organizations they run the risk of losing not only the legitimacy gained from them, but the resources acquired from northern NGOs.

When they meet demands made by northern NGOs in order to obtain resources, southern NGOs often sacrifice their autonomy. This has critical implications for these NGOs' role as development agents and for their contribution to a strong, association-based civil society – the cornerstone of a healthy democracy.

Southern NGOs' boards of advisors or trustees should serve as a mediator between the competing and conflicting demands of grassroots groups on the one hand and northern NGOs on the other. However, this has generally not been the case. These boards have been weak or under-utilized, and have often existed in name only. The lack of a public philanthropic tradition necessary to recruit, utilize, and maintain board members further constrains southern NGOs in this area. When they do recruit and retain board members, southern NGOs very seldom know how to use them, and often lack the skills to engage the board and to follow its strategic direction. Sometimes disregard for the board is deliberate. Many southern NGOs are founded and led by one or two dynamic individuals who set up a board to please donors, but actually resent any intrusions. These leaders may feel they are undermined by the board, and may sabotage any attempts by it to impose checks and balances on their power. Quite often, the board does not establish the southern NGO and hire its executive staff, but, rather, the leaders of the southern NGO select the board. This process shifts the balance of power to the southern NGO leaders, and undermines the role of the board.

This chapter has outlined the framework of interorganizational influence, which posits that organizational behaviour can be understood only in the context of an organization's environment. Organizations acquire resources from the environment in order to survive, so the appropriate starting point for an analysis of organizations is to find out how they gain resources, not how they use them. Interdependence characterizes an organization's transactions with the environment, and the concepts of sensitivity and vulnerability suggest the extent to which an organization is subject to the influence of the actor holding the resource, and the degree to which it will be subject to external control.

Altering relationships between northern and southern NGOs is difficult, since the problems between them are essentially political, not organizational. This is one of the reasons why capacity-building initiatives have often failed to strengthen southern NGOs relative to northern NGOs. Capacity-building activities do not address the root of the problem: the unequal distribution of power between northern and southern NGOs is a result of the unequal distribution of resources between them.

Changing relationships between northern and southern NGOs is not impossible. The first step is to view these relationships not as a zero-sum game in which there are winners and losers, but as interdependent. Altering northern NGOs' relationships with southern NGOs can benefit northern NGOs by increasing their development effectiveness. It can benefit southern NGOs by increasing their ability to work responsively and flexibly with development beneficiaries, rather than making them respond to the directives of northern NGOs and their donors. And, ultimately, this will benefit the recipients of development assistance, since these activities will address their own needs as they have identified them. NGOs of any type will only realize their contribution to democracy when they strengthen the voice of the poor and marginalized, those who are the intended recipients of development assistance. Until NGOs empower these groups, their only contribution to democracy will be by proxy.

4   Paying the Piper and Calling the Tune: Northern NGOs' Capacity-Building Support for Southern NGOs

So what if southern NGOs are dependent on northern NGOs for resources, and the nature of northern NGOs' support subjects southern NGOs to external control? Why does this matter? And, more importantly, what can be done about it?

As the framework of inter-organizational influence developed in the previous chapter suggests, southern NGOs' resource dependence places them at a distinct disadvantage with respect to northern NGOs. North–south NGO relationships have been characterized by northern NGO dominance and southern NGO subservience to the conditions which northern NGOs attach to their support.

This chapter argues that in order truly to enhance southern NGOs' capacity and ability to contribute to civil society development, northern NGOs must do two things:

1   They must shift the focus of capacity building from one which strengthens internal organizational aspects to one which addresses external variables, such as southern NGOs' ability to forge relationships with the organizations which can provide resources.
2   They must reconfigure their own structures, procedures and operations so that they are more responsive to southern NGOs. This in turn will enable southern NGOs to be more responsive to community groups.

Capacity Building

What is capacity building? In short, it is the process by which northern NGOs try to strengthen southern NGOs so that they become more sustainable organizations and are better able to carry out programmes. Table 4.1 provides an overview of the range of northern NGOs' approaches to developing southern NGOs' capacity and, ultimately, supporting civil society.

Narrowly defined, capacity-building initiatives focus on the provision of material and/or technical support which will enable southern NGOs to carry out their immediate goals of project-related services or, increasingly, advocacy. Capacity building encompasses material, financial, and human resource development. Capacity building in this sense is seen as an end in itself rather than a means to any other end. In this view, support for southern NGOs is a justifiable goal in its own right. Examples of this type of capacity-building support include providing NGO staff with training in the areas of: project design and management; accounting; and report writing, monitoring, and evaluation.

The drawback of this type of assistance is that it often focuses on strengthening southern NGOs' financial management capabilities so that they can handle large sums of foreign money, or on strengthening their administrative capabilities so that they can carry out donors' and northern NGOs' operational activities. In short, capacity building of this type strengthens southern NGOs' ability to carry out northern NGOs' and donors' agendas, rather than their own.

At the other end of the spectrum are those initiatives which treat southern NGOs purely as a means to achieving broader ends. Southern NGOs are supported not because of their presumed comparative advantage in delivering development services, but because they are seen as an appropriate vehicle for strengthening civil society. It is not southern NGOs' work *per se* which is of value, but rather their perceived ability to feed into wider societal processes. NGOs are strengthened as a way to develop a vibrant associational life, in which a plurality of interests are represented and a wide range of people participate in policy and decision-making processes. Capacity-building support in this area may include regional or national networking activities, advocacy training, or even support for

Table 4.1 Goals of northern NGO capacity-building interventions

	Capacity building as means to broader end	Capacity building as process	Capacity building as end in itself
Capacity enhancing for the NGO	The focus of this intervention is on the outcomes, not the set of activities undertaken to achieve them or the methods used to effect changes. The overarching concern here is that the NGO has a strengthened and sustainable position *vis-à-vis* the broader context within which it exists.	A broader view of capacity enhancing achieved by an understanding of the means through which organizational change may be most sustainable. This may occur in the course of capacity enhancing of NGOs (as a means or as an end) or of civil society. It refers more to the method undertaken to achieve the desired outcome.	A very narrow conception of capacity enhancing, whose focus entails attention to the structures and functions of the NGO; general concern is for efficiency, rather than the overall effectiveness or appropriateness of the mission.
Capacity enhancing for the NGO sector	The goal of these interventions is the creation of a strong and vibrant democratic culture where norms and values have been successfully inculcated, and the procedures and rules have been successfully established. To achieve these ends, interventions may focus on organizations very different from those whose capacity enhancing is a means. For example, attention may be given to the judiciary, electoral bodies, and voter registration groups.	Encouraging actors in civil society to engage in debate, and to challenge and/or support the existing regime. Educating the general public as to its rights and responsibilities as citizens. Facilitating people's ability to make claims on government and to open channels for recourse where infringements of rights occur.	This intervention is concerned with enabling various sets of organizations to achieve their desired aims and objectives, since they are viewed as a legitimate contribution to a flourishing, association-based civil society. The organizations are the means through which this is achieved; therefore capacity enhancing entails a concerted effort to strengthen them. In this conceptualization, the sector is viewed in the aggregate rather than as component parts.

Source: Adapted from Bebbington and Mitlin (1996)

NGOs' core costs like office space, salaries, and overhead costs.

Many donors have adopted this type of approach erroneously, thinking that support for southern NGOs can be equated with strengthening civil society. Capacity building for southern NGOs contributes to civil society development only when it results in southern NGOs which are able to:

- increase citizens' ability to articulate their interests through either participatory development projects or lobbying and advocacy activities;
- respond to people's most pressing needs as they identify them;
- increase social capital through the formation of networks and collective action which serves as a counterbalance to entrenched political and economic interests.

James (1994) identified the following priority areas for capacity-enhancing initiatives. Listed in decreasing order of prevalence, according to northern NGOs' initiatives with southern NGOs, they are:

1 giving partners increased power in the partnership relation;
2 using supportive financing methods;
3 providing institutional funding;
4 supporting management training;
5 encouraging organizational development consultancy;
6 providing management advisors/staff attachments;
7 supporting the development of southern networks;
8 supporting southern training/consultancy research centres.

Only the last two approaches, the least common, focus on improving the organizations' relationship with the external environment. While the first approach may appear to address external concerns since it focuses on altering existing relationships, it does not address the more fundamental issue of which actors an organization should interact with based on how the organization interprets and enacts its external environment. Contextual factors such as these have been excluded from capacity-enhancing initiatives, and therefore, northern NGOs' assistance to southern NGOs has not enabled the latter to work with their beneficiaries in a way which would contribute to civil society development.

Africare/USA discovered the difficulties of trying to support civil society development through capacity building for southern NGOs when it evaluated its Benin Indigenous NGO Strengthening (BINGO) programme. This initiative had as an explicit goal promoting governance and democratization. The project operated under the assumption that the strengthening of NGOs as a class of social actors contributes to these processes. Specifically, supporting Benin NGOs was seen as a means to achieving participatory grassroots development activities and to enabling NGOs to channel and respond to grassroots groups' demands.

Although its efforts to support NGOs advocating free and fair elections directly addressed governance issues, Africare found that the project was less successful in linking governance and democratization interventions to the rest of the project. Recommendations to improve this situation included encouraging internal democracy within an NGO, and actively promoting collaboration between NGOs and governments.

Africare had two goals with respect to the BINGO project:

1   creating an 'ideal' type of southern NGO, which other southern NGOs would accept and emulate;
2   strengthening democracy and providing economic and political access to grassroots groups.

It was this second, broader purpose which '... legitimized the intervention, and ultimately it is the economic and political development of these populations which will define the impact of the project'. The evaluation determined that this broader goal was 'overambitious' in what it proposed to achieve in three years, and that it was unable to link its capacity-enhancing initiatives with democratization.

Capacity Building Critiqued

Part of the problem with defining or operationalizing capacity-building interventions is that the term is inherently relative.

An organization seeking to build another's capacity must first assess the latter's capabilities and then determine which ones need to be improved. Alternatively, NGOs which request capacity building can undertake self-assessments in order to determine where their specific needs are and then identify which organization would be appropriate to assist them. CRS, INTRAC, and the United States Agency for International Development (USAID) are among those that have developed organizational self-assessment tools to help their NGO partners identify capacity-building needs.

INTRAC suggests five questions which are common to organizational assessments, and these give some indication of the general areas in which capacity-building interventions might be directed. The recipient organization should answer these before a programme of capacity-building support is embarked on:

1   What is our organization's purpose in society?
2   For whom are we here?
3   What do the people we are here for value or find important?
4   What are our results?
5   What is our plan?

The majority of capacity-enhancing initiatives are neither an end in themselves nor a means to a broader end, but are largely *ad hoc*, one-time provisions of support, often undertaken with little sense of how this will contribute to an immediate goal, much less a broader one of strengthening civil society. Quite often these approaches are not even grouped under a heading of capacity building *per se*.

Perhaps the most helpful way of thinking about northern NGOs' support to southern NGOs is to divide it into three categories:

1   those interventions designed to assist a southern NGO as an organization;
2   those designed to assist a southern NGO's programme performance, particularly with respect to grassroots groups;
3   those designed to strengthen a southern NGO's relation-

ships with the external environment, that is those organizations and actors which provide resources or legitimacy essential to the southern NGO's existence.

The last category is the most important, yet most often overlooked in capacity building. If northern NGOs want to strengthen southern NGOs' capacity, then they need to focus less on southern NGOs' internal weaknesses, such as accounting and project-management skills, and more on the skills which would equip southern NGOs to extract resources from the external environment without jeopardizing their autonomy and in the process their credibility.

Southern NGOs' organizational capacity has largely been measured by how effectively they use resources, and capacity-enhancing initiatives have been structured to enhance southern NGOs' ability to manage resources, account for them, and distribute them to client groups. Overall, capacity enhancing has concentrated on the internal components and dynamics of organizations, rather than their exchanges and relationships with actors in the external environment. Southern NGOs' ability to obtain resources depends on how well they acknowledge, assess, and address their external environment, since this produces the relationships which will supply the necessary resources.

But it is not just any relationship which will counter southern NGOs' resource dependence. The nature of the relationship must be such that southern NGOs are assured of their funding and are able to use it with a certain degree of discretion in order to respond to communities' needs. Uncertainty and control by northern NGOs, however, characterize most North–South NGO relationships. In order to enhance southern NGOs' capacity and to decrease their vulnerability to external control, capacity-enhancing initiatives must focus on changing an organization's environment as well as its internal elements.

Northern NGOs are the key actors in southern NGOs' external environments; therefore, changes to northern NGOs' structures and operations would benefit southern NGOs, since they would favourably alter the way in which the latter are able to interact with their environment, and it would help to decrease the uncertainty associated with that environment, which ultimately subjects southern NGOs to external control. According to Pfeffer and Salancik (1978: 278):

> If organizational actions are responses to their environments, then the external perspective on organizational functioning argues strongly that organizational behavior is determined through the design of organizational environments. The focus for attempts to change organizations, it would appear, should be the context of organizations. By changing the context, the behavior of the organizations can be changed. The profoundly important topic of designing organizational environments is almost completely neglected. The idea of changing organizations by changing their environments is scarcely found in the literature on organizational change.

Since few northern NGOs offer southern NGOs funding to cover their operating costs, the latter generally seek assistance from the former for specific projects. The uncertainty associated with this type of funding makes it very difficult, if not impossible, for southern NGOs to operate strategically. They are unable to plan their activities or allocate staff time and other organizational resources beyond the projects which northern NGOs have funded. Even when they know that they have the money, the time lag between the northern NGO actually approving a project and that money being transferred may jeopardize southern NGOs' ability to carry out their work.

Northern NGOs, therefore, may enhance southern NGOs' capacity by changing themselves, by altering the way in which they decide how to use resources, allocate resources, and account for resources. By altering their own structures and operations, northern NGOs could also reduce to some extent the uncertainty attached to their provision of support.

For instance, reducing the delay between funds being awarded and southern NGOs receiving them would enhance southern NGOs' capacity to respond to grassroots groups in a timely manner. Or changing donor funding cycles to accommodate farming calendars would ensure that community groups received critical inputs like seeds and tools or credit when they needed them, rather than when it suited the organizational bureaucracy.

In some cases, northern NGOs could enter into relationships

with particular southern NGOs which have a proven track record and links with community groups to provide long-term, guaranteed financial assistance to cover core costs and other administrative overheads. This would release the southern NGOs from the uncertainty surrounding their existence and ability to work with community groups, and enable them to concentrate on the development work at hand, while planning for sustainability after the northern NGOs' support has ended.

The lack of untied resources which southern NGOs command hinders their ability to respond to communities' needs by facilitating grassroots development projects initiated by the communities rather than donors, and reacting flexibly to ever-changing local conditions brought on by economic and political instability. The way in which northern NGOs channel support to southern NGOs and the nature of their relationships undermine southern NGOs' greatest contribution to the development process: their knowledge of the social and cultural considerations which so influence the outcomes of development interventions.

ARD, for example, worked with one village group to sink a water well, using money from a northern NGO. ARD met with the villagers and the chief to discuss where the well should be dug. The chief felt that it should be dug in front of his house so that he could monitor its use and ensure that animals were kept away from it and that small children did not fall into it.

ARD, however, met with women in the village, since they are primarily responsible for collecting water, and asked where they felt the well should be dug. After much discussion, the women acknowledged – rather reluctantly because of their respect for the traditional authority – that they did not want the well in front of the chief's house, since they would have little privacy there.

ARD discovered that while the women collected water, they liked to talk, discuss their husbands, their children, village life. This informal interaction provided them with support, strength, and solidarity: evidence of the social capital which distinguishes a healthy civil society. Sinking the well in front of the chief's house might have eroded this social capital since the women would no longer have been able to talk openly as they worked. ARD's sensitivity to local norms demonstrates how it can engage with community groups to ensure the effectiveness of development interventions. Yet few northern NGOs were willing to give ARD the control over resources or decision making which would enable it to do so.

Generally, northern NGOs provide support to southern NGOs through grants and contracts. Grants give the most latitude to field operations, since money is awarded to achieve a certain goal and the process by which that goal should be achieved is left to the discretion of the grant recipient. Grants are increasingly scarce, particularly small grants, since northern NGOs' overhead costs for administering these are prohibitive in the light of decreasing foreign aid budgets and resulting staff reductions. More often, contracts are awarded which specify, usually in great detail, the work to be done and how it should be accomplished.

One striking and defining characteristic of northern NGOs' approaches to capacity-building support for southern NGOs is that it very often reflects a one-way notion of this endeavour. Seldom, if ever, is there any discussion of what southern NGOs offer to northern NGOs in this process. CARE is one exception to this general rule. When considering collaboration with a southern NGO, CARE asks what the southern NGO can do for it. While CARE does this to avoid a 'paternalistic' approach, it also forces the southern NGO to define its comparative advantage, that is what it does best and what it brings to the exchange relationship.

Oxfam America also displayed one of the more enlightened, and realistic, approaches to capacity-enhancing initiatives when it pointed out that some of the more sophisticated southern NGOs with which it works 'understand that we depend on them as they depend on us' (CARE, 1994: 14). World Neighbors/USA also reflects the importance of its southern NGO counterparts by defining 'partnership' as a 'co-learning relationship'. The southern NGOs (and other local counterparts with which World Neighbors works) provide the organization with access to networks, indigenous knowledge, language skills for broader networking, and on-the-ground opinions about the context within which World Neighbors works (CARE, 1994: 31).

Save the Children Fund/USA (SCF/USA) recognizes the importance of southern NGOs (and other local partners) to a significant extent by requiring managers to include partnering and institution-building goals in their annual operating plan (CARE, 1994: 9). Part of the reason that SCF/USA emphasizes capacity enhancing of southern NGOs is that it wants to reduce its own staff of 3,000 employees and it sees handing over programme responsibilities as one potential strategy for decreasing the scale of its operations while still retaining impact (CARE, 1994: 3). As bilateral assistance budgets are cut and northern NGOs seek out new, cost-effective approaches to development work, capacity-building initiatives become increasingly popular. CRS/USA is a good example of this. Given the uncertainty of CRS's continued presence in some of the countries in which it works, it has adopted a strategic approach to capacity enhancing in order to prepare local organizations to take over programmes should it withdraw.

In addition to serving northern NGOs' bureaucratic needs, capacity building can be enormously profitable for them. In some cases, it may be of more benefit to them than to southern NGOs. As former President Nixon once said of American aid, 'remember that the main purpose of American aid is not to help other nations but to help ourselves' (cited in Opeskin, 1996: 21). A significant portion of the resources intended for southern NGOs' capacity-building assistance returns to northern NGOs through grants or contracts for training and consultancies, or it goes to businesses for fax machines, vehicles, and other equipment normally purchased outside developing countries.

Capacity Building and Donors

The politics of North–South NGO relationships and the respective roles of each in setting the development agenda have been of increasing concern to donors and multilateral organizations which are eager to strengthen southern NGOs' capacity. For example, USAID's New Partnerships Initiative (NPI), introduced at the World Summit for Social Development in 1995, aims to advance USAID's existing sustainable development goals through building grassroots capacity and enhancing national enabling environments.

The NPI has as one of its goals to build the capacity of

southern NGOs. One of the three core components of this programme is encouraging NGO empowerment. To this end, USAID missions have been charged with a responsibility to 'pursue opportunities to support the development of local NGOs' (USAID, 1995: 16). Since USAID will work with northern NGOs and donors to accomplish this, it has encouraged, even mandated, those working in collaboration with it to share this goal.

The NPI distinguishes between USAID missions that use NGOs as service providers without enhancing their sustainability or capacity and those that have a concern for the latter. USAID, through the NPI programme, has adopted this policy: 'Where appropriate, USAID will incorporate into procurement and assistance documents provisions requiring implementors to strengthen the institutional capacity of local NGOs. This in turn will become a principal criterion for judging performance' (ibid.).

The NPI carves out a significant role for northern NGOs that work with southern NGOs. One of its goals for building southern NGOs' capacity is to create and sustain an extensive network of 'partnership' relationships, which would include links between USAID and northern NGOs, northern and southern NGOs, and USAID missions and southern NGOs. In order to encourage these relationships, USAID will, through NPI, rely on northern NGOs' judgement and expertise. This means that, in theory, northern NGOs will be integrally involved in programme activities and have increased input into USAID planning and decision making (USAID, 1995: NGO Empowerment Section, ii). USAID contends that, 'Positive results [for capacity building] have been obtained through partnerships between stronger and weaker organizations' (ibid. i–13).

The World Bank has also undertaken 'NGO partnership building activities'. For example, in one community-based food-security project the Bank conducted in Benin (Gopal and Marc, 1994), northern NGOs were paired with southern NGOs as 'project partners' to try to encourage the transfer of methodologies and technology. In this role, northern NGOs were obliged to help southern NGOs upgrade their capacities in the area of project design and administration. By the end of the World Bank project the southern NGOs were to be self-sustaining. Northern NGOs were paid for services rendered. The Bank provides training to southern NGOs that have the potential to contribute to Bank projects or advocacy work, but lack the capacity to do so. Generally, this training is provided by a special component of technical assistance built into a large project, or through a separate project. For example, the Ethiopia Social Rehabilitation Fund invites NGOs to submit proposals for identified training needs. The project has designed community development and micro-project development training to meet these needs, and has appointed a training and promotion officer.

A very different case is the Bangladesh Second Road Rehabilitation and Maintenance Project. In this instance, the task manager identified the need for the NGO working with the Bank to receive training in the use of the Bank's resettlement guidelines and generally in land valuation and compensation. While this is just one of many examples of the Bank's efforts to provide training, it does raise the pertinent and pressing issue of whether or not NGOs' capacities should be improved in certain areas, since they appear fundamentally at odds with beneficiaries' priorities. It also demonstrates clearly how capacity building is used to strengthen the donors' ability to carry out their agendas, rather than the NGOs' ability to develop and implement theirs.

Efforts to address the politics of north–south NGO relationships through partnership arrangements often fall short, since operations lag behind the policy changes, and this is where southern NGOs feel most disempowered. African NGOs reflected their exasperation with the power inequalities inherent in relationships when they said during a conference, 'It's useless to talk about these issues. Just tell us what we have to do to get the money.'

Redressing the imbalance between northern and southern NGOs, and altering their relationships so that southern NGOs can more easily obtain resources and exercise discretion over those resources, will increase the effectiveness of development interventions and as a result serve both northern and southern NGOs' interests. Northern NGOs will be able to obtain money from donors on the basis of their positive results, and southern NGOs will have better relationships with community groups, since they will be responding to the latter's needs rather than those of donors. Ultimately, the community's enhanced ability to articulate and respond to its own needs will contribute to the development of a vibrant civil society.

5 Cascading Conditionalities and the Role of International Organizations in Capacity Building

Many northern NGOs are aware that their assistance to southern NGOs constrains the latter's ability to respond to grassroots groups. These northern NGOs would like to change the nature of their relationships with southern NGOs to give the latter more control of resources and decision making. They would like to enhance southern NGOs' skills in fundraising and other activities which would enable southern NGOs to interact more strategically with the external environment and to counter their resource dependence. Most northern NGOs are acutely aware of southern NGOs' reliance on them and the ways in which this subjects southern NGOs to external control.

But in many ways northern NGOs are powerless to change. They receive resources from the organizations in their external environment, such as bilateral donors and multilateral organizations, and this assistance comes with its own conditions, conditions which northern NGOs pass on to southern NGOs. In short, northern NGOs often have little room to manoeuvre in their work with southern NGOs.

This chapter examines the role that the United Nations and the World Bank play in shaping northern NGOs' relationships with southern NGOs, and how these organizations have altered the politics of North–South NGO relationships by their increased involvement with southern NGOs. This has significant implications for southern NGOs' capacity, and this is discussed here.

NGOs' Evolving Relationships with International Agencies

NGOs' changing roles in development and their reliance on the external environment for resources have created new alliances between NGOs and international organizations like the United Nations and the World Bank. Such relationships yield opportunities as well as obstacles for NGOs.

In many ways, collaboration between international organizations and any type of NGO seems implausible. NGOs by definition are non-governmental, even though the increasing amounts of official assistance they receive have confused this distinction. The United Nations and the World Bank deal primarily with governments. The United Nations is an intergovernmental body comprised of member nations, and the World Bank is a government-owned international financial institution which loans money and provides technical assistance to governments.

In addition to their very different structures, NGOs and international organizations have different natures. NGOs are perceived to be small, flexible, innovative, and responsive to beneficiaries, while the United Nations and the World Bank are known as large, complex institutions beholden to the bureaucracies which created them. Overall, the different organizational histories, cultures, approaches to development, staff members, and resource bases have led to varying degrees of conflict and tension over the years. These same factors have also led to varying degrees of interdependence.

Historically, the United Nations and the World Bank have involved NGOs in their operations in a number of areas and at a number of levels, ranging from field operations to dialogue at headquarters. The starting point for the United Nations' relationship with NGOs is Article 71 of the UN Charter. This provides the UN Economic and Social Council (ECOSOC) with the mandate to establish consultative arrangements with NGOs. ECOSOC Resolution 1296 was adopted in 1968, and this provides a three-category system of NGO recognition with different privileges of consultation accorded to each category. Category I organizations are large, representative bodies working on a wide range of topics. Category II includes organizations with skills in only some of the ECOSOC issues. Finally, organizations listed on the Roster are those which can make occasional contributions to the work of the Council.

In addition, 1948 saw the establishment of the Conference of Non-Governmental Organizations (CONGO) in Consultative Status with the Economic and Social Council. This coordinating body serves as a watchdog of NGO interests and provides a framework for NGO cooperation in fields of common interest.

Starting in 1972, NGOs intensified their interaction with the United Nations system by participating in the United Nations Conference on the Human Environment in Stockholm. NGOs held an NGO Forum parallel to the official conference and produced an NGO daily newspaper which shed light on details of the negotiations. Without NGO participation much of the conference dialogue and debate on issues would have been less open to public scrutiny.

Subsequent conferences such as the Second World Women's Conference in 1985 in Nairobi, the 1992 Conference on Environment and Development in Rio de Janeiro, and the 1995 Fourth United Nations Women's Conference in Beijing saw a marked increase in the involvement of NGOs. Most notably, organizers actively sought out NGO involvement rather than grudgingly giving them space. In fact, NGOs' role has become so great that, some have observed, 'it would now be inconceivable for the UN to plan any global event without the active involvement of the non-governmental sector' (Rice and Ritchie, 1995: 256).

NGOs and the World Bank

The World Bank has traditionally dealt with two types of international and national NGO: those engaged in operational activities, and those involved in advocacy work. Because many NGOs fall somewhere between these categories or increasingly engage in both types of activity, the distinction between the two is now less clear than it has previously been.

NGOs are important to the World Bank, just as the World Bank is important to many NGOs given its political leverage and its control over a significant amount of development resources. Bank policies favouring associations with NGOs include an Operational Policy Note in 1981, an Operational Directive (OD 14.70) in 1989, and a Good Practice in 1997 (GP 14.70). In general, NGOs contribute to World Bank operations, policies, research, and analyses. NGOs offer:

1   skills and contacts that further the Bank's mission of environmentally sustainable poverty reduction;
2   alternative analyses of development issues;
3   influence among decision makers and the public, particularly in donor countries;
4   input into all stages of operational projects, starting with their design;
5   input into country assistance strategy formulation and consultations on major new policies, including, for example, those related to structural adjustment, the environment, Bank governance, and social policy.

Similarly, the Bank contributes to NGOs by providing:

• opportunities for collaboration and dialogue with their governments;
• resources for expanding successful development projects;
• information relevant to development strategies;
• impetus for governments to support a more enabling environment for NGOs' work.

Between 1973 and 1988, 6 per cent of Bank-financed projects involved NGOs. In 1993, over one-third of all approved projects included some form of NGO involvement. By 1994 this percentage had increased to one half. Realizing the practical importance of involving southern NGOs in some sectors of its operations, and in response to advocacy NGOs' concerns, the World Bank in 1988 made an institution-wide effort to expand its work with NGOs.

The World Bank's strategic interaction with NGOs began in the early 1980s with the establishment of the NGO–World Bank Committee. Since the Bank had increasingly engaged in poverty-focused activities, it required NGOs' input to some of these projects in a variety of sectors. The committee was established to examine the emerging collaboration with NGOs. In recent years, the committee has been overhauled to reflect the range of interactions between NGOs and the Bank, to construct more appropriate forums for policy debate, and to guide the Bank's evolving NGO strategy.

NGO–World Bank interaction gathered momentum and public attention between 1991 and 1992, when several groups of NGOs sought to influence the 10th International Development Association (IDA) replenishment. The IDA makes loans or gives 'credits' to the world's poorest countries unable to afford regular World Bank terms. Donor countries replenish the IDA as part of their overseas development assistance (ODA). In fact, it has been said that the World Bank initially engaged with NGOs essentially as a public relations exercise, since the World Bank was concerned that NGOs' criticisms of its operations would threaten its funding. For their part, NGOs worked with the World Bank because they hoped to influence donor governments to make changes in its information policy, poverty and structural adjustment lending, and energy and water-sector policies.

Limitations to NGOs' Influence

NGOs' increased interaction with the World Bank has not necessarily translated into increased influence over its activities or policies. A review (Nelson, 1995) of 304 World Bank projects which involved NGOs between 1973 and 1990 assessed the nature of NGO involvement, the character of the NGOs involved, and particularly the growth in the number of projects with NGO involvement since 1988. Of these projects, only 76 featured interaction with NGOs where the NGOs were engaged beyond project implementation. These projects were unusual since they involved NGOs in project design, included direct funding of NGO projects by a Bank-financed fund, or involved conflict between the Bank's project managers and NGOs over the outcomes of the projects. These 76 projects represent the most intensive project interaction to date, and the kind of interaction which the Bank claims to want with more NGOs.

Given the constraints of formal interaction with NGOs, the United Nations and the World Bank have also cultivated informal linkages, in part because their need for NGOs' services has been changing more rapidly than official policies and procedures can accommodate. Through informal interactions and influence, NGOs are increasingly responsible for shaping policy rather than simply providing information or services. For example, many NGOs with representatives in New York are more active in the UN General Assembly than they are in ECOSOC. Several subsidiary bodies of the General Assembly have created informal arrangements by which NGOs can circulate documents on the floor of the Assembly. And, while NGOs do not have formal representation with the UN Security Council, they have influenced its activities in a direct way through their capacity to alert the media to situations and to sway public opinion. One example was the way in which humanitarian NGOs such as Africa Watch in Washington, Médecins Sans Frontières in Paris and Brussels, and Oxfam and Africa Rights in the UK prompted an international response to the war in Rwanda.

Overall, NGOs' relationships with the United Nations and the World Bank have shifted in three significant ways. First, there is a concerted attempt by the United Nations and the World Bank to involve NGOs in areas beyond project or programme implementation. International agencies are seeking more substantive collaboration with NGOs for two reasons. As chapter 1 discussed, NGOs are seen as vehicles of democratization and civil society development, goals to which most donor governments now subscribe. In addition, the dominant development ideology is predisposed towards state disengagement, privatization, competition, and grassroots participation. NGOs are believed to be integral to the success of this agenda since they can fill the gaps left by government retrenchment, encourage private enterprise, and involve beneficiaries in development activities.

Second, NGOs are often viewed now as the preferred channel for collaboration rather than as temporary partners to be used only when government capacity is weak. Former UN Secretary-General Boutros Boutros-Ghali told NGO representatives in 1994, 'I want you to consider this your home. Until recently, these words might have caused astonishment. The United Nations was considered to be a forum for sovereign states alone. . . . [NGOs] are now considered full participants in international life' (cited in Rice and Ritchie, 1995: 256).

There are reasons why NGOs should view such statements with a healthy scepticism. As Doug Hellinger (1989: 33) of the Development Group for Alternative Policies (commonly known as the Development GAP) pointed out in the context of the World Bank's work with NGOs:

> It is important to remember that the stimulation for much of the institution's recent interest in NGOs has been its need to mitigate some of the worst effects of its own lending without having to alter its loan portfolio or the speed at which money is allocated and disbursed to highly indebted countries. NGOs might find it difficult at times to determine, for example, whether they are being used to carry out small-scale, showcase environmental projects in countries in which wide-scale ecological damage is being done as a consequence of Bank lending or, similarly, being asked to deliver social services and small-scale credit packages while government social service budgets and credit programs are being gutted as a condition of Bank adjustment loans.

NGOs may find that the United Nations and the World Bank have embraced their work simply because NGOs provide these agencies with an opportunity publicly to support development efforts geared towards the poorest groups, while at the same time retaining policies which worsen their condition. In spite of this danger of co-optation, NGOs continue to engage with the United Nations and the World Bank, since the relationships provide them with resources, recognition, and in some cases an opportunity to influence programmes and policies.

The third, and perhaps most significant, change in international organizations' work with NGOs is that more southern NGOs have been able to participate in dialogue or even in project and policy work, a role generally reserved for northern NGOs. Quite often these relationships are brokered by northern NGOs, but as southern NGOs acquire the skills and experience needed to engage directly with international organizations, they have started to resent the northern NGOs' role.

In fact, as the United Nations and the World Bank actively seek input and collaboration from national and local NGOs, some staff members are beginning to question northern NGOs'

credibility and legitimacy, charging that they do not necessarily represent national or local NGOs' concerns, and that it
makes more sense to work directly with the national or local
organizations. This has altered the politics of North–South
NGO relationships, since southern NGOs suddenly have more
clout *vis-à-vis* powerful international organizations, and northern NGOs must increasingly interact with southern NGOs if
they want to receive resources from these organizations.

Moreover, as the United Nations and the World Bank
engage directly with southern NGOs they discover the organizational weaknesses which constrain southern NGOs' work,
and as a result have prioritized capacity building for southern
NGOs. This has encouraged, and in some cases forced, northern NGOs to shift from an operational role to a facilitative one,
in which they work with southern NGOs to increase their
capacity to carry out development projects, a role they carry
out to the specifications of the organizations providing
the resources and setting the agenda. The United Nations and
the World Bank shape northern NGOs' relationships with
southern NGOs, since they often provide resources for
capacity-building work with southern NGOs, or inform bilateral donors' agendas, therefore influencing the priorities and
programmes they support. The following two sections discuss
each of these issues in turn.

Politics of NGOs' Relationships with International Organizations

The United Nations and the World Bank have altered the
politics of North–South NGO relationships by engaging
directly with southern NGOs, since this has shifted the power
paradigm in the latter's favour. But southern NGOs still find
that much of the capacity-building support they receive, either
in conjunction with a particular project or as an end in itself, is
administered by northern NGOs. Southern NGOs, therefore,
are reliant on northern NGOs, which in turn must answer to
the organizations providing the resources.

In addition, both northern and southern NGOs' political
nature becomes more pronounced when they engage with the
United Nations and the World Bank, since NGOs' work

becomes more visible and their impact is potentially greater, given the magnitude of international agencies' policies and programmes. NGOs are no longer addressing development problems at the community level. They are looking toward the meso and macro level and trying to effect change in the structures which constrain their community-development initiatives. This process often leads to conflict, particularly with government leaders or other powerful, entrenched interest groups.

By encouraging accountability to poor groups, NGOs may challenge the sovereignty of governments. As a result, when international agencies work with these NGOs, the former may jeopardize their privileged relationships with governments. For example, the World Bank's mandate allows it to interact with NGOs only with the consent of governments, and all activities undertaken must conform to a government's policies toward NGOs. Governments often resent the projects or the capacity-building support that the World Bank channels to NGOs, charging that at worst many of these NGOs are really opposition parties and threaten government stability, and at best they fail to coordinate and integrate their development work with government programmes.

Government sovereignty is more often challenged when international agencies work with advocacy NGOs than when they collaborate with NGOs involved strictly in service delivery. One of the sectors where this is most apparent is human rights. For example, the UN Working Group on Arbitrary Detentions reported in 1995 that 74 per cent of the cases it took up in 1994 were brought by international NGOs and another 23 per cent came from national NGOs. The remaining 3 per cent came from families (Gaer, 1995: 393). This means that NGOs are integral to the success of the United Nations' human rights work. In fact, it has been said (ibid. 389) that 'human rights NGOs are the engine for virtually every advance made by the United Nations in the field of human rights since its founding.'

Many governments, however, resent the activities of human rights NGOs in spite of their reliance on these organizations for information. Governments criticized by NGOs may lobby to limit their formal access and participation, and try to cast doubt on the legitimacy of their findings. The United Nations and the World Bank may find themselves in the middle, caught between the governments which provide their finance and direct their operations and the NGOs upon which they increasingly rely to make their activities more effective, sustainable, and legitimate.

NGOs are not necessarily engaged in a zero-sum game, trying to further the cause of one group at the expense of another. Rather, as NGOs struggle to represent the interests of the poor and the marginalized, they provide politicians and international agencies with an opportunity to gain favourable publicity by responding to the needs of these groups once the NGOs have made them public. As NGOs and governments clarify their relationships and work together, governments' concerns that NGOs represent a political threat may lessen, and as many authoritarian regimes are replaced by new democracies, the new regimes may be more open to NGO involvement.

Implications of Changing Relationships for Southern NGOs' Capacity

Southern NGOs' changing role with respect to international organizations increases their capacity in two ways. First, it enables them to obtain resources and recognition from these powerful and influential organizations. Second, as the World Bank and the United Nations shift towards working directly with southern NGOs, this strengthens southern NGOs' position with respect to northern NGOs, and challenges the latter to redefine their own role in the development process.

Southern NGOs can exploit new avenues for funding by working with the United Nations and the World Bank. This helps southern NGOs to counter their lack of resources and enables them to work with their beneficiary groups. For example, southern NGOs can receive project funds from the World Bank by serving as paid consultants or contractors to either borrowing governments or the Bank.

In selected cases, other bilateral or multilateral agencies co-fund NGOs' activities. The World Bank does not directly fund NGOs but rather makes loans to governments for them. In addition, there is a handful of special programmes which allow the Bank to grant NGOs small amounts of money for specific purposes. These include: the Small Grants Program; the Special Grants Program; the Safe Motherhood Special Grants Program; the Population NGOs Special Grants Program; the Small and Medium Enterprise Pilot Initiative; and the Global Environmental Facility Small Grants Program.

The World Bank and the United Nations have increasingly sought out southern NGOs in project and policy work, and to inform their research and analyses. In addition to the capacity-building funds and training opportunities which they have provided, both the United Nations and the World Bank have sought to enhance southern NGOs' role by selecting appropriate partners among them, working with the resident missions, whose staff members have greater knowledge about which NGOs would make the best partners, and increasing flexibility in contracts and procurement so that southern NGOs are able to obtain the resources that they need.

In addition, the World Bank has emphasized the importance of the enabling environment for NGOs, and has encouraged governments to examine their relationships with NGOs and the legislation which guides this to ensure that it is not unnecessarily restrictive and affords NGOs the space they need to carry out development interventions.

The selection of southern NGO partners is a critical issue since, too often, international agencies are drawn to NGOs which have computers, vehicles, English-speaking staff, and other trappings that may make collaboration convenient, but which do not have any commitment to communities. There is no shortage of dubious NGOs staffed by career opportunists concerned more with making money or travelling overseas than with supporting disadvantaged communities.

Southern NGOs' capacity may be increased by their relationships with international agencies, but, on the other hand, many NGOs find that the labyrinth of bureaucracy that they must negotiate in order to obtain these resources actually hinders their organizational capacity. NGO staff may find it difficult to fulfil the demands of the organizations while remaining responsive to beneficiary groups. They may also discover that they need to use a significant portion of their limited resources to communicate with these agencies, entertain their staff members on field visits, and complete reports to their satisfaction.

NGOs with limited capital reserves may not be able to operate on the expense-reimbursement cycle which is often standard procedure for international organizations. Failure to provide up front the resources that NGOs need may hinder their ability to carry out their work effectively. Such was the case with the World Bank's Indonesia Yogyakarta Rural Development Project. One of the local NGOs contracted by the World Bank to construct water-storage containers was unable to complete construction or pay the local labourers for their work owing to delays in the disbursement of project funds.

In addition to taxing their already limited capacity, relationships with the World Bank and the United Nations may undermine NGOs' lobbying and advocacy powers, since multilateral organizations are an integral part of the international system that NGOs are trying to reform. In some cases, NGOs' relationships with the United Nations and the World Bank may diminish NGOs' credibility at the field level among groups which have been adversely affected by the policies and programmes that these organizations support. The NGOs' legitimacy is then at stake.

In spite of these obstacles, it is imperative that NGOs engage with international organizations. NGOs often represent local communities' only opportunity to influence international agencies' policies and programmes, and in the process change local conditions. As Sollis (1992: 174) observes, 'The question therefore is no longer "What will NGOs do if they find themselves in a position of relating to the multilateral associations (MLAs)?" On the contrary, the most pressing issue for NGOs is to prepare for engagement with MLAs and the when, why, how, and what of the relationship.'

This willingness to work with other institutions while maintaining independence and critical distance has been referred to by Stephen Commins (1996: 4) of World Vision as 'critical engagement'. Such engagement must be based on trust, and involve listening to and learning from conflicting points of view.

Critical engagement can contribute to the development of a global civil society which reflects and supports transnational concerns rather than narrow, state-centric or ethnic/nationalistic-based interests. Many environmental NGOs have provided a good example of how consensus and community can be built around common issues, even when common ground is lacking.

NGOs are uniquely positioned to facilitate the development of a global civil society in which state behaviour becomes less central to collective choice. Most bilateral donors have realized that their development assistance has in some cases been thwarted by an inefficient or corrupt state, one which was overly involved in its economy. NGOs have played a significant role in stimulating and supporting civil society development. They can challenge powerful organizations such as the United Nations and the World Bank to respond to poor or disadvantaged groups which may not have access to these institutions. Likewise, NGOs can work with community groups to help them organize, articulate their needs, and identify and implement solutions. NGOs' ability to interact strategically with diverse actors in the external environment provides them with their distinct competency for strengthening civil society. By making connections between state and non-state actors, rich and poor, donors and recipients, the powerful and powerless, NGOs are helping to promote understanding of the global system, an understanding which can ultimately lead to its transformation.

6 Sierra Leone and The Gambia: Case Studies of NGO Interdependence

Case studies of relationships between northern and southern NGOs provide a clear picture of the asymmetry in exchange relationships and how this imbalance leads to external control. NGOs in Sierra Leone and The Gambia have relied on the external environment for resources to such a degree that the entire NGO sector in these countries is largely donor driven and reflects outside interests rather than those of grassroots groups.

Given the poor political and economic climate in Sierra Leone and The Gambia, and the resulting limited infrastructure and resources, NGOs in both these countries are perhaps extreme cases and therefore not broadly representative of the experience of NGOs in all developing countries. However, it is because southern NGOs' resource dependence is so pronounced in these environments that they offer a useful illustration of the effects that this has on their operations, their relationships with northern NGOs in the external environment, and their ability to assist grassroots groups.

The following sections explore in detail four southern NGOs, tracing their relationships with northern NGOs and the effect that these have had on the southern NGOs' capacity and ability to assist grassroots groups. Of the four, only one was able to manage its relationships with actors in the external environment in a way which enabled it to retain a degree of autonomy. The concluding section discusses why.

The Cases of ARD and OREINT in Sierra Leone

Sierra Leone's political and economic scene has suffered from gross mismanagement, corruption, and abuse, culminating in the crisis of a collapsing state. Government failure to provide social services, particularly for the rural population, has created space for southern NGOs to work in Sierra Leone. Persistent and progressive economic deterioration has limited the government's ability to act and constrains southern NGOs' opportunities for local resource mobilization, thus requiring them to seek resources from northern NGOs.

ARD was established to assist grassroots groups, and to ensure that northern NGOs' development projects were appropriate for the culture and context within which they were operating. To achieve these goals, ARD developed two arms of operations:

1   promoting grassroots development through working with grassroots groups;
2   performing consultancy services for northern NGOs.

ARD, however, has always lacked the capital required to undertake its own projects with grassroots groups, so its resource dependence has meant that it must pursue the latter of the two functions. Initially, ARD saw consultancy services as a way of earning income to support the first function. ARD soon found that these activities took up all of its time, and that the resources generated from them only covered basic overhead costs associated with running the organization.

ARD does not initiate village development projects, but responds to requests for assistance from communities already undertaking development work, or from northern NGOs interested in supporting particular projects. ARD outlined its priority areas as: fostering food self-sufficiency; improving health and nutrition; small enterprise development with an emphasis on women's groups and activities; and training workshops and seminars. ARD selects for further collaboration the most viable grassroots groups from its register. It assists these in obtaining resources from northern NGOs and donors. Initially, it used the following criteria for selecting grassroots groups for further collaboration:

1 degree of village interest;
2 accessibility from towns;
3 existence of organized farmers' groups;
4 presence of strong, organized women's groups;
5 success rate of past development projects;
6 proximity of market place;
7 dynamism of local organization;
8 involvement of local leadership.

Later as ARD developed, the criteria for accepting membership organizations for further collaboration were as follows:

1 visit by an ARD official;
2 clear and measurable objectives;
3 good track record;
4 easy access;
5 high potential for viability;
6 high level of group participation;
7 clear benefits for the community;
8 some training in development management;
9 links with other organizations.

The implications of this shift are that ARD seemingly contradicted its original mandate of working with the poorest of the poor and the most marginalized groups, particularly those in out-of-the-way places, away from main roads. ARD's criteria seemed to reflect its desire to work with groups which would produce results pleasing to donors, were easy to reach, and had already undergone some degree of organizational development support or training. These were not likely to be the poorest or most marginalized.

ARD's register of grassroots groups details their sources of support, and this log reveals that ARD was unable to provide direct assistance to any of the groups registered with it. Instead, it evaluated groups according to northern NGOs' criteria. If ARD recommended a group for funding, the northern NGO either sent it directly to the group or channelled the assistance through ARD. Either way, ARD's resource dependence meant that it worked on the terms and conditions established by the northern NGOs. ARD's executive director summarized the predicament it faced, saying:

One of the constraints we encounter is identifying whose agenda is respected in the field. Is it that of the northern NGO or the southern NGO? Too often, aid is tied to conditionalities. 'Here is the money, but it must be spent on this.' Is this healthy, considering that the realities in the field may dictate otherwise?

Although ARD currently claims more than 200 grassroots groups in its database, only 136 groups are listed in the draft of the 1994 ARD annual report. Out of the 136 listed groups, ARD recorded interaction with 110. Interaction means either visiting the project, evaluating it for northern NGOs, advising it for them, or linking it with them. Out of these 110 groups, 98 received funding from northern NGOs, 12 have funding applications pending with them, and 8 had their funding requests rejected by them. The draft annual report records that ARD visited only 24 of the 136 groups registered.

This low number of visits, however, may not be an accurate representation of ARD's involvement with grassroots groups, since appraisal reports exist for groups that ARD does not list as having been visited. In recent years, rebel attacks have made travel to rural areas unsafe, and this has limited ARD's ability to reach its registered groups. ARD has endeavoured to visit groups in areas that were relatively unaffected by rebel attacks. It is worth noting that while ARD has stated as its explicit goal the building of grassroots groups' capacity, nowhere does it define what exactly this entails.

ARD's relationships with grassroots groups are its principal means of financial security, since it receives from northern NGOs fees for services rendered. This source of funding is not dependable, since ARD is never in a position to determine the number of assignments allocated over a period of time. ARD is constrained by its own internal weaknesses, such as lack of technical expertise or training, but underneath these internal problems is a more fundamental and long-overlooked constraint: the absence of resources.

In order to counter its resource dependence, ARD has turned to northern NGOs for capacity-enhancing support to help sustain its operations on the one hand, and to reach its registered groups on the other. Applying the framework of inter-organizational influence to ARD's relationships with northern NGOs reveals that these relationships were characterized by vulnerability interdependence and, as a result, ARD was subject to external control.

One of ARD's first international partners was Oxfam UK, which has provided direct grants to ARD (including a small fund to support micro-projects), funds for training membership organizations, and payment for evaluation services rendered. The money from the grant covered ARD staff salaries and other administrative costs such as office renovations. Oxfam also allowed ARD to invest part of the grant money provided in Sierra Leone government treasury bills, in order to generate interest which could be used to finance ARD programmes and administrative costs. In addition to appraising ongoing or potential Oxfam-funded projects, ARD took over responsibility for directly supervising and disbursing funds for the Mabaykaneh Agricultural Project, which Oxfam had approved for two-year funding during the 1991/92 financial year.

Oxfam was unique in that it provided ARD with institutional support at a very early stage in the relationship. This was mostly due to the fact that Oxfam was closing down its operational presence in Sierra Leone and needed local counterparts who could gradually take over its functions, thus making sure that Oxfam's withdrawal was not too abrupt or disruptive for the groups that it had supported. By increasing ARD's capacity, Oxfam was assured that the work it had started would continue.

Although ARD appears sensitive to Oxfam, since other organizations could, and often did, provide similar assistance, it was in fact vulnerable to Oxfam given the magnitude of the exchanges. Again, this magnitude is measured by assessing the proportion of total inputs or the proportion of total outputs accounted for by the exchange, that is how significant this exchange is with respect to all others. In October 1992 ARD summarized this in correspondence by saying, 'Apart from Oxfam/UK, no other partner has ever assisted us with increasing our institutional capacity. . . . This is how we have been able to cope for the past 1½ years.'

Even after ARD received support from other northern NGOs, the Oxfam contribution accounted for a significant proportion of ARD's total inputs. Therefore, ARD remained vulnerable to Oxfam. Oxfam was vulnerable to ARD (but only in the context of its work in Sierra Leone) because after 1990 the organization had ceased to have an operational presence in the country and relied on ARD to advise its projects, report to it on progress, and account for money spent.

Bread for the World/Germany contributed to ARD's organizational development by providing ARD with block funding to conduct pre- and post-funding appraisals of membership organizations' projects. To increase ARD's logistical capacity and ability to make site visits, Bread for the World donated a Toyota Land Cruiser, and funds to cover spare parts and running expenses for one year. Bread for the World also provides a training fund for ARD to facilitate workshops for membership organizations covering issues such as report writing, development and management, and agro-forestry.

In a particularly innovative move, one that reflects the trust that has been built between the organizations over a period of several years, a Small Project Fund was established by Bread for the World to be administered by ARD. The introduction of this fund to Sierra Leone enabled ARD to have more control over which grassroots groups received assistance, and to have influence over the types of project undertaken. The advantages of setting up the fund include:

1 timely response to small requests from groups which do not require funding above the ceiling amount agreed on;
2 immediate allocation of funds to groups beginning their activities, especially those that are seasonal and dependent on the farming calendar;
3 possible reduction in the number of applications sent to Bread for the World, thus reducing administrative tasks;
4 flexibility on the part of ARD and the Small Project Fund committee to consider viable projects that meet the established criteria.

The exchange with Bread for the World was again one in which ARD appeared sensitive, since it could receive the support elsewhere, but was actually vulnerable given the magnitude of the exchange. ARD relies only on Oxfam, Christian Aid and Bread for the World for institutional and programming financial support. This meant that the Bread for the World funds were a significant proportion of the total inputs ARD received. Bread for the World was sensitive to ARD, since Council of Churches Sierra Leone (CCSL) also provided services to Bread for the World, and was actually considered as its primary in-country partner.

Christian Aid provided ARD with a block grant to monitor and evaluate projects it funded throughout Sierra Leone. ARD budgeted one visit every three months for each of the nine projects that Christian Aid initially asked it to monitor. Each of these visits lasted two or three days. On such trips, ARD reviewed project records, accounts, and field activities and provided technical or managerial assistance where possible. In addition, Christian Aid also provided the salary for a female projects officer.

In 1991, Kanja Sesay and Alie Forna were hired by the African Development Foundation (ADF) to serve as resident evaluators in Sierra Leone. In this capacity, they were responsible for assessing three ADF-funded projects. While the ADF work did not directly benefit ARD, it provided the founder members of ARD with salaries, and heightened the organization's profile locally and internationally. Sesay and Forna participated in numerous ADF-funded conferences throughout Africa, and these networks have increased ARD's contacts with development professionals there.

Given the income that ARD received from ADF and the lack of other sources to provide it, ARD was vulnerable to ADF. ADF was also vulnerable to ARD given the way the relationship was structured. While ADF had a country representative, it relied on the resident evaluators to gather data on its field projects. Through an interview and selection process it was determined that ARD was the most appropriate partner, thus suggesting that it would be difficult if not impossible for ADF to receive the services from elsewhere. Presumably other candidates did not have the development background and skills that Sesay and Forna possessed.

By initiating a relationship with ARD, CUSO/Sierra Leone boosted ARD's credibility and visibility, since CUSO was one of the first northern NGOs in Sierra Leone to work with ARD. This relationship gave ARD entry into the International NGO Forum meetings, and enabled it to take a key role in publishing

NGO News, a local newsletter on NGO activities published out of CUSO's office. CUSO also funded a Post-Harvest Loss Minimization Workshop for small farmers, which ARD facilitated, and provided ARD with a portable generator to facilitate their operations when there was no electricity, or when they were conducting workshops in villages where there was no power.

CUSO was vulnerable to ARD, since its headquarters mandated it to work through southern NGOs, and at the time the relationship with ARD was forged there were few, if any, other suitable organizations with which it could work. ARD was only sensitive to CUSO, since it could gain legitimacy through its work with other organizations, which could provide the funds for training and generators.

Other northern NGOs gave ARD assistance in the form of one-time provision of material resources. Development and Peace/Canada provided ARD with a Toyota pick-up truck for use as a farm-input delivery van when transporting materials to membership organizations. The University of Dayton, Ohio, provided a computer and laser printer, and Project Extend/ USA granted US$3,000 for ARD to help cover office renovation and daily administrative costs. However, the Project Extend money was held in a BCCI account and was lost when the bank folded amidst the scandal of 1991. CUSO provided a portable generator, and an anonymous donor also provided a more powerful, non-portable model for running the computer and office equipment. These relationships were characterized by sensitivity interdependence on both sides, since they were not critical resources for the southern NGO, and the northern NGO did not gain considerably from the exchange.

OREINT

The organization for Research and Extension of Intermediate Technology (OREINT) was established in 1984 to promote appropriate technology in Sierra Leone's rural areas. It set out to work through grassroots groups, and to this end developed different categories of OREINT membership. These are outlined in the organization's constitution as:

- national grassroots association network members;
- national volunteers for environment and development;
- founder members.

The first category consists of those groups which have registered with OREINT. They are eligible to receive information, resources, and technical assistance. The second category is made up of Sierra Leonean professionals and technicians who lend support or financial assistance to OREINT's work with grassroots groups. Founder members are those who have significantly contributed to the establishment of the organization.

OREINT aims to enhance grassroots groups' technological capacity through work in five programme areas: agricultural innovation, small enterprise development, appropriate technology, community development, and environment and development. OREINT has liaised with northern NGOs and donors to obtain the necessary resources to execute several projects with grassroots groups. As in the case of ARD, the groups that OREINT has been able to reach are the ones that northern NGOs identify and decide to support, rather than ones that OREINT has identified based on its own criteria. Like ARD, it has shifted from working as an operational organization to serving as an intermediary for northern NGOs, carrying out projects of their design with groups of their choice, rather than implementing OREINT projects with OREINT's selected groups.

OREINT's relationships with grassroots groups are determined by northern NGOs because it lacks its own resources to develop and carry out projects with them. Its primary project is the Kamaworni Agricultural Project (KAP) funded by the International Development Fund of the Universities of Chalmers and Göteborg in Sweden. KAP is a membership organization founded in 1986 with the aim of achieving food self-sufficiency and improved living standards for its members. The International Development Fund supplied US$20,450 for KAP to purchase seeds and basic farm tools. Given the initial success of the seed revolving scheme, the project was expanded to include six other member villages.

OREINT co-implements the project on behalf of the donor agency. OREINT's responsibilities include assessing the project for the International Development Fund at the universities, and designing and planning activities with the community. The universities send an evaluator once a year to monitor progress.

OREINT's interaction with the project appears limited, particularly since KAP is situated in a remote and – during the rainy season when the roads wash out – often inaccessible area of the country. In 1992 OREINT visited the project four times. It also conducted a workshop with project participants to train them in basic project management and implementation skills. As a result of OREINT's intervention with the project, additional needs were identified and subsequent projects approved on the basis of those recommendations.

OREINT's relationship with the universities is vulnerable given the magnitude of the exchange. Measured against its other relationships with northern NGOs, it is clear that this one accounts for the greatest proportion of OREINT's total inputs. OREINT has few other ongoing, financed activities with groups that enable it to build its reputation at the grassroots level. Without the universities' funds, it would not be able to reach the groups. The universities are sensitive to OREINT, since they can carry out their work with grassroots groups irrespective of OREINT's contribution.

Another organization which has supported OREINT's work with grassroots groups is the Rabobank Foundation in The Netherlands. OREINT requested financial assistance on behalf of the Gbom Kargbo community group. As a result, the group received money to improve its food security and to construct a store. OREINT provides monitoring, evaluation, and training services to the group and sends progress reports to the Foundation. However, because the Foundation does not allow for administrative costs, OREINT receives no overhead support for its role in coordinating the project. The Foundation provides the assistance directly to the group. Although OREINT established the relationship with the group, the project is carried out under the terms established by the northern NGO, since it is providing the assistance.

OREINT's relationship with the Rabobank Foundation is characterized by sensitivity on the part of the Foundation and vulnerability at OREINT's end. The foundation is sensitive, since the activities that OREINT assists are not critical to it; in fact, it has ceased supporting projects in Sierra Leone because of the political instability there. OREINT is vulnerable given the magnitude of the exchange and its lack of other opportunities to work with grassroots groups. Since it has so few other northern NGO partners and opportunities to work with membership organizations, its relationship with the Foundation accounts for a significant proportion of OREINT's total outputs with grassroots groups.

The Sierra Leone office of CAUSE Canada has also worked with OREINT. OREINT assessed the technical capacity of a soap-making project in the Waterloo refugee camp, and designed a standard store for CAUSE Canada's post-harvest programme in rural areas. CAUSE Canada provided OREINT with power backup for its computer and a battery charger. This assistance is funded with a grant from CIDA. CAUSE Canada said that its present relationship with OREINT was undertaken to increase that organization's capacity, and that the specific assistance will depend on requests from OREINT.

However, CAUSE Canada claims it has limited capacity to support OREINT even though it deems that organization's activities relevant to Sierra Leone's development. While no formal relationship agreement currently exists, CAUSE Canada said that the future of the relationship would depend on each organization's needs. The interdependence that has resulted from the organizations' interaction is one of mutual sensitivity, since other organizations could provide CAUSE Canada with technical assistance, and OREINT could either exist without the resources that CAUSE Canada provides or obtain them elsewhere.

PLAN International in Sierra Leone has worked with OREINT since 1985. It is the second most significant actor in OREINT's external environment, providing OREINT with funds for technical and vocational training, and fees for technical assistance. PLAN International, however, is a northern NGO based in Sierra Leone, and for that reason its transactions with OREINT are less likely to be uncertain than those of the universities in Sweden.

OREINT has assisted PLAN International's work with grassroots groups by providing technical assistance, and support in project implementation, monitoring, evaluation, and coordination. PLAN International contracts OREINT to carry out these services. The terms of the relationship are specified in the contract, and to date, the interaction has not expanded beyond this. According to PLAN International, it contributes to OREINT's capacity by using a number of OREINT's diverse services on a regular basis. This enables OREINT to earn money and gain experience in these areas. PLAN intends to continue to strengthen the relationship in order to build OREINT's capacity. OREINT's interactions with PLAN are grouped under the year in which they occurred. They are as follows:

1 *1985*: designed and monitored an integrated model village with the development of biogas digester; promoted extension of animal husbandry and irrigation using bio-fertilizer for rice farming; introduced fast-growing tree crops and improved wood stoves;

2 *1988–9*: monitored appropriate water and sanitation construction works for rural Western Area;

3 *1991*: trained trainers for family life orientation for PLAN Foster Families in rural Western Area;

4 *1993*: conducted household survey in one of PLAN's urban operational areas;

5 *1994*: conducted an evaluation of PLAN Makeni integrated health project;

6 *since 1994*: coordinating technical and vocational training for unemployed males under one of PLAN's urban programmes;

7 *1995*: conducted an assessment of the impact of seed input assistance to farmers in 40 villages of the rural Western Area;

8 *1995*: assessed the feasibility of the Bayconfields Cooperative Market Centre as an income-generating project.

The relationship between PLAN International and OREINT is one of vulnerability interdependence on both sides, since PLAN International relies on the technical advice that OREINT provides in order to ensure the success of its projects. There are no other southern NGOs in Sierra Leone dedicated to providing information and assistance on technology. By working with a southern NGO, PLAN gains local legitimacy and credibility in Sierra Leone, and with its donors. OREINT relies on PLAN for the income provided for these services, and the credibility and track record it establishes through working with both a northern NGO and grassroots groups.

The Cases of GARDA and GAFNA in The Gambia

It is within the context of a resource-dependent nation, struggling with economic reform programmes and political transitions, and vulnerable to external shocks and manipulations, that NGOs have emerged to provide development services in The Gambia. According to Davis et al. (1994: 253) decentralization in the 1980s and early 1990s in The Gambia has been achieved by NGOs, which have grown rapidly in number and significance. Given recent cuts in international aid generally, and assistance to The Gambia specifically, NGOs' initiatives are increasingly important.

GARDA

The Gambia Rural Development Agency's (GARDA's) long-term objective is to help rural women improve their socio-economic well-being and become self-reliant. GARDA works to meet this objective through the following goals:

- to assist the poorest households, especially the most disadvantaged groups;
- to improve the agricultural productivity and income levels of rural households;
- to provide assistance in the form of cash credits for production and processing inputs, storage facilities for cereals, and income-generating activities;
- to provide assistance for the protection and preservation of the environment with particular emphasis on maintaining a sustainable natural resource base (GARDA, 1993: 1).

GARDA became operational in 1988–9 and carries out its activities in collaboration with community groups in the

Lower River Division (LRD) and the North Bank Division (NBD). GARDA links community groups with northern NGOs in order to acquire financial support for activities such as vegetable gardening, cereal banks, petty trading and micro-enterprise development, credit, and beekeeping. GARDA supports all facets of grassroots groups' project-related work, including management.

CRS was one of the first northern NGOs to support GARDA. From the very early stages of the GARDA–CRS relationship, however, the latter defined the terms. According to GARDA's leader, Kebba Bah, 'As we started the development partnership, they [CRS] came down with their conditions.' CRS's response to GARDA's initial project proposal suggested that GARDA had weaknesses and that CRS could address its weaknesses. Later, it became evident that while GARDA benefited from the relationship, CRS did so too, since it needed southern NGOs which would use its money appropriately, serving as success stories and evidence of the effectiveness of its capacity-enhancing assistance.

By working with GARDA, CRS increased its access to community groups, its performance, and its accountability to headquarters and donors, who emphasized the importance of building southern NGOs' capacities.

The relationship between CRS and GARDA was marked by vulnerability interdependence, since CRS needed GARDA to fulfil its mandate of working through local organizations, and GARDA needed CRS's resources to enable it to reach groups at the field level.

CRS could not legitimately justify its presence in The Gambia if it did not have local capacity-building projects, since that is the organization's global strategy. While CRS had other southern NGO partners in The Gambia, they were not as exemplary as GARDA. GARDA, on the other hand, could exist without CRS's support, since its legitimacy in the field did not rely on the credit programme that CRS supported.

GARDA also received capacity-building support from the West Africa Rural Foundation (WARF), an international grant-making NGO with a West African governing board and staff concerned with rural development in the sub-region. WARF funded and conducted in 1994 a 'Diagnosis for GARDA's Institutional Strengthening'. On the basis of a five-day visit with GARDA, interviewing staff and board members, WARF concluded that GARDA's major weakness was 'the absence of planned intervention'. WARF recommended that GARDA receive training in long-term planning based on participatory community needs assessment.

Since WARF's concern is for long-term capacity building and institution building of local organizations as opposed to project implementation, it identified GARDA as a viable organization with which it could work in The Gambia. In this way, WARF's and GARDA's relationship was one of interdependence, since WARF needed to disburse funds to reliable organizations in order to justify its existence to its donors, the Ford Foundation and the International Development Research Centre. For its part, GARDA depends on organizations like WARF for assistance covering core costs. However, if WARF were to withdraw its funding GARDA could approach other donors, whereas WARF was rather limited in its choice of viable southern NGOs in The Gambia that would make effective use of funding. Given this, WARF was vulnerable to GARDA (in the context of its Gambian operations) while GARDA was sensitive to WARF.

Impressed by GARDA's field activities and positive track record of channelling support to community groups, the Irish Agency for Personal Service Overseas (APSO) agreed to assist GARDA's capacity building by addressing its logistical needs. APSO is a national agency funded by the Irish government which places Irish volunteers in developing countries as technical assistance personnel. APSO/Ireland agreed to provide GARDA with a vehicle and motorbikes to help GARDA travel throughout its operational base. APSO/Gambia also agreed to provide two technical volunteers to work with GARDA in the field for two years. APSO's assistance differs from that of CRS and WARF in that it is not part of a larger capacity-building strategy, but a discrete intervention intended to enhance GARDA's organizational capacity. Many northern NGOs favour this type of interaction with southern NGOs, since it is less expensive and time consuming.

APSO and GARDA are interdependent, since APSO relies on GARDA to absorb its volunteers and GARDA needs the support that APSO is willing to provide. The interdependence is one characterized by sensitivity on both sides, since APSO could send its volunteers to any number of other countries or organizations. GARDA could also exist as it has done without transport, or it could identify another donor to meet this need. And GARDA could continue without the addition of technical volunteers.

Indirectly, GARDA's relationships with northern NGOs contribute to its organizational capacity by providing funding that allows it to undertake projects with community groups, and to build the positive track record which is essential for garnering support. These northern NGOs also link GARDA into international networks and provide credibility to the organization through their association with it, since they are more established and often have positive name recognition. For this reason, GARDA and the organizations providing project-related support are interdependent.

GAFNA

The Gambia Food and Nutrition Association (GAFNA) provides maternal and child health support at the village level, and is increasingly concerned with conducting nutrition education programmes which use traditional leaders to communicate messages in innovative ways. GAFNA is quite possibly the best-resourced national NGO in the country, given its long-term relationship with CRS.

GAFNA was formed in 1986 by a group of senior development workers in NGOs and government who were concerned about malnutrition in The Gambia, and the lack of coordination among groups dealing with the problem. GAFNA's goal was to ensure that there was no duplication, or over-concentration, of efforts in one area, and to keep NGOs from operating without controls. Although GAFNA was initially an association of members without a secretariat to oversee its efforts, it did have a governing body which was responsible for the running of the organization. The governing body held annual general meetings and yearly workshops on topical issues.

Between 1986 and 1988 GAFNA's main role and primary achievement were to serve as an umbrella body for health and nutrition professionals and projects in The Gambia. GAFNA served to coordinate activities between government ministries, between NGOs, and between the government and NGOs. During this period, it drew development money to The Gambia, since donors were attracted to GAFNA's relationship with the government and its ability to coordinate health and nutrition interventions.

GAFNA offers membership to interested individuals and organizations concerned with nutrition, and uses members' fees to supplement support from external agencies. Categories of GAFNA membership include institutional, individual, and life. A wide range of Gambian and international agencies are GAFNA members, including the United Nations Development Programme (UNDP), the World Health Organization (WHO), Unicef, CRS, SCF/USA, the Medical Research Council, the Ministry of Health, the Ministry of Agriculture, and the Department of Community Development. Members of good standing have the right to vote on issues pertaining to GAFNA at general meetings.

GAFNA evolved to its present form as a result of CRS's desire to address malnutrition in The Gambia, which is a serious development problem particularly for pregnant and lactating mothers, and children under five. CRS sought collaboration with GAFNA in order to assist GAFNA's organizational development and to help it obtain resources. CRS viewed GAFNA as an NGO which had nutrition expertise and indigenous knowledge that could help CRS restructure its programmes to reflect community needs and practices better. Indeed, many people have suggested that CRS was responsible for the creation of GAFNA as an operational development organization. CRS handed over to GAFNA the operational/administrative aspects of implementing its main health and nutrition programme, while CRS remained responsible for providing financial and management assistance, particularly related to all aspects of the PL 480 Title II food aid that USAID gave to the project. (PL 480 Title II is a US assistance programme that gives surplus agricultural commodities as food aid, either for use or for monetization.)

GAFNA's main programme is the Health and Nutrition Institutional Support Program (HNISP), which it carries out with support from CRS and in collaboration with the government. The broad goal of the HNISP is to improve the nutritional status of rural Gambian women and their children. Three general objectives follow from this goal. They are:

- to enable Gambian organizations to assume a dynamic and creative role in designing and implementing long-term health and nutrition interventions;
- to enable pregnant and lactating women in rural areas to improve their own health and nutritional status and that of their children, as measured by reduced incidence of low birthweight babies and malnutrition in children under two years old;
- to promote the use of local foods in health and nutrition interventions while simultaneously phasing out imported food aid used for the same purpose.

According to GAFNA records, the HNISP targets approximately 25,900 pregnant and lactating women with children up to two years of age. Pregnant women enrol in the programme after being referred either by their traditional birth attendants, or by the Ministry of Health's Maternal and Child Health programme. Participating mothers attend monthly health and nutrition education sessions at the centres, and receive an imported food supplement. Community health nurses or trained traditional birth attendants deliver the education component. The 119 centres are managed by all-female Community Management Committees (CMCs), made up of traditional village leaders and traditional birth attendants drawn from villages where the centres are located. Record keepers assist the CMCs with secretarial services such as registering participants and preparing monthly reports.

The HNISP is GAFNA's primary link with rural communities, and the way in which it is directed by CRS and USAID limits GAFNA's ability to respond to community groups' concerns about its implementation. Given that the HNISP monopolizes GAFNA's staff time and that the resources it receives from CRS are earmarked for the HNISP, GAFNA is unable to engage in other meaningful activities with community groups in response to community groups' needs or demands.

CRS monitors GAFNA at two levels: financially and operationally. GAFNA must submit a financial report to CRS each month so that the latter can check for over-expenditure. GAFNA's programmes are also evaluated by CRS to ensure that they are in line with GAFNA's stated objectives. Every year GAFNA submits a progress report to CRS, which it evaluates against set benchmarks, and then sends in the form of a progress report to USAID, since CRS must account to USAID for funding received for the HNISP.

CRS auditors monitor food distributed at the HNP centres and ensures the local communities' contribution has been made since it is ultimately responsible for accounting to USAID. It is GAFNA's responsibility to ensure that the CMCs manage the centres according to the guidelines laid out in a CRS management manual, which adheres to USAID funding conditions. CRS gets monthly reports from the centres on the use of commodities and finances, and will not supply food to centres whose reports are submitted with a delay of more than two months. The interruption of food supplies results in a *de facto* suspension of the centre until all outstanding reports are submitted. According to USAID Regulation 11, if there is a loss of more than US$500, CRS must file a claim against that centre and suspend its operations. Out of 119 centres, 17 have had claims filed against them. Nine of these are now repaying the money that was lost. CRS relies on GAFNA to use traditional means of communication in meetings with the CMCs to learn what constraints they are facing and how these can be addressed.

CRS also conducts end-use checks every quarter on GAFNA's field staff, and requires monthly reports of activities. This posed problems, since GAFNA staff felt that they did not have time to complete these evaluations and maintain their work with the communities. So CRS held a workshop to address the situation and to try to plan activities better so that field officers would have more time for reporting. The GAFNA secretariat is also evaluated annually, and salary increases depend on performance that year.

CRS's direct involvement in the programme may be the reason behind the frustration, lack of ownership, and low morale that GAFNA staff express when discussing the HNISP. Since CRS must account to USAID for the food and finances provided for the programme, CRS oversees GAFNA's work with the CMCs. A senior staff member of GAFNA said that without CRS pressure no work would get done. A GAFNA staff member said that, 'If CRS doesn't sit on us, we don't deliver.' GAFNA staff used to produce quarterly reports for CRS but now only complete them annually. Other documents stay in draft and are never finalized, including one that was still in draft from 1992. CRS's HNISP supervisor in Banjul said that:

> GAFNA doesn't like the idea that we're always banging on their door. We want to make sure that all the programmes we planned are achieved. If CRS says to USAID that x tons of food will be used and x number of women will be fed, then we need to meet these targets. So CRS puts pressure on GAFNA. CRS needs to justify the huge amount of money spent on GAFNA administration. . . . We push GAFNA for efficiency. We want results, impact. If USAID bangs on our door asking for impact, we bang on GAFNA's door asking for impact.

CRS's work with GAFNA has been described as offering it financial viability and discipline. Financial discipline enabled GAFNA to attract donors, since it could produce the audited books and orderly accounts that donors sought to ensure their 'investment' would be secure. GAFNA's efforts to find donors have not been altogether successful. It has raised 20 per cent of its funds, the target amount set by CRS, but it lacks income-generation activities or donors willing to support the organization on a long-term, institutional-development basis. It has suggested that CRS create an endowment and donate the interest to it; and; it has suggested purchasing its own office building so that in the long term money would be saved on office rent.

One of GAFNA's senior staff said that the organization has not successfully secured outside sources of funding because on the one hand it is a difficult undertaking, and on the other GAFNA has not tried hard enough and the organizational capacity is lacking. It was said that the organization is complacent because it has relied on CRS for so long, and that while GAFNA's director is searching for other funds, he is not pushing the organization hard enough to be self-reliant. By its own account, GAFNA spends the majority of its time with the HNISP, so it is difficult to undertake other projects and find donors for them. Finally, because GAFNA is the only national NGO concerned with nutritional issues that has an established track record and organizational capacity, most of its projects have been handed to it, which has meant that it has had little experience designing a project and soliciting funds.

The relationship between CRS and GAFNA is one of interdependence, since CRS relies on GAFNA to implement its food and nutrition programme, and since it can fulfil its mandate of working with southern NGOs through its institutional support to GAFNA. GAFNA relies on CRS for nearly all of its operational and capacity-building support. The relationship is characterized by vulnerability on both sides, since without GAFNA CRS could not effectively carry out the programme or continue receiving support from USAID to fund it. Without CRS, GAFNA could no longer exist, since it lacks its own financial base and other secure donor support.

One of GAFNA's secondary projects is a Village Water Hygiene and Sanitation project it took over in 1991 from WaterAid International, a Rotary-funded organization, which closed its operations in The Gambia. According to GAFNA, this project aims to improve the water and environmental conditions in villages by reducing the incidence of water-borne and other related diseases. When the project was handed over, it had a two-year life span with funding coming from Rotary International. GAFNA reports that with the project, it inherited six field staff and some equipment, and that the staff have assisted GAFNA's work by creating awareness in villages of the need for improved refuse disposal and the use of safe latrines. Staff have also trained participants to coordinate project activities in their own villages. This project complements the HNISP, since it aims to improve sanitation, thus decreasing infections and enhancing nutritional status.

In March 1992 GAFNA undertook a three-year Fruit and Vegetable Processing and Preservation Project in collaboration with VillageAid/UK (a northern NGO) and the Food and Nutrition Unit in the Ministry of Agriculture, in order to decrease post-harvest loss and to enhance nutrition levels. The project collected excess fruit and vegetables and preserved them, with a view to marketing them. Women were to benefit from the proceeds they earned selling produce to the project, and families' nutritional status was to improve through the increased access to fruits and vegetables. GAFNA field staff report, however, that it proved impossible to preserve the produce for longer than one month, so the project provides added-value only from the processing of the fruit and vegetables.

Other community activities that GAFNA has carried out include:

- weaning food promotion, funded by a USAID project called Primary Health Care Technologies (PRITECH);
- a pilot interactive nutrition education campaign funded by the Gambia Government/World Bank Women in Development project;
- a knowledge, attitudes, beliefs, and practices study on maternal feeding during pregnancy and lactation, also funded by The Gambia Government/World Bank Women in Development project (GAFNA, 1992: 12).

UNIDO funded GAFNA to conduct a training programme for women entrepreneurs in the food-processing unit, and to produce a training manual suited to The Gambia. A small-scale enterprise specialist was seconded to GAFNA from Unido.

GAFNA's relationships with external agencies assist its work at the community level, and provide capacity-enhancing support for it as an organization. By far the most important external relationship it has is with CRS. However, while other partnerships are currently peripheral to GAFNA's operations and organizational support, relationships of these types are central to its future and sustainability. CRS covers 80 per cent of GAFNA's operational budget. CRS had covered 100 per cent of GAFNA expenditures and then set it as a goal that GAFNA should raise 50 per cent of its own finance from sources outside CRS and USAID. However, GAFNA was unable to achieve this goal and the figure was lowered to 20 per cent of its own financing by 1995. GAFNA achieved the 20 per cent goal by levying 7 per cent of total project costs against both VillageAid and WaterAid for running their respective projects, and by raising 8 per cent from GAFNA membership funds.

GAFNA's relationships with VillageAid and WaterAid are interdependent, since it relies on these organizations to cover a portion of its operational expenses, and the organizations rely on GAFNA to carry out their programmes. The relationship is characterized by vulnerability on GAFNA's side and sensitivity on the part of VillageAid and WaterAid. GAFNA is vulnerable, since the organizations provide the percentage of core costs that CRS has required GAFNA to raise. Without these funds, it would be entirely reliant on CRS and unable to fulfil its agreement with that organization. VillageAid and WaterAid are sensitive to GAFNA, since they can exist without the projects that GAFNA executes on their behalf.

Conclusions

In short, GARDA was the only southern NGO in the four case studies able to manage its relationships with northern NGOs in a way which enabled it to work with community groups on their terms, and which provided the organization with the resources necessary for survival.

Although ARD had a significant number of relationships with northern NGOs, their nature actually transformed ARD from an operational organization into an intermediary working for northern NGOs. Capacity-enhancing initiatives increased ARD's ability to carry out northern NGOs' mandates, rather than to carry out its own.

In other words, the outside interventions undertaken by northern NGOs did not improve ARD's performance in relation to its mission, context, resources, and sustainability; ARD did not have an increased ability to acknowledge, assess, and address its external environment. However, northern NGOs – as a result of their interventions with ARD – had improved performance in relation to their mission, context, resources, and sustainability; the northern NGOs had an increased ability to acknowledge, assess, and address the external environment in Sierra Leone.

OREINT's resource dependence prompted it to seek relationships with northern NGOs that would increase its capacity and provide it with opportunities to work with grassroots groups. These relationships rendered it vulnerable, since their number and nature were such that two – those with PLAN and with the universities in Sweden – account for a significant proportion of OREINT's total inputs or outputs with grassroots groups. In other words, if one of these partners dropped OREINT, the overall operation of the organization would be in jeopardy, since it lacks other relations of substance which could serve as a buffer against the uncertainty and provide the required resources.

While the number of OREINT's relationships with actors in the external environment proves problematic for OREINT's capacity, the nature of the relationships has also hindered it, since they have not addressed its long-term organizational development needs. OREINT has received no core funding to sustain its organization, and it does not have long-term partners willing to serve as a source of support.

Factors Influencing GARDA's Success

The GAFNA case provides an interesting contrast to the others, since it has one northern NGO partner rather than many. GAFNA illustrates how northern NGOs may, however unwittingly, subject southern NGOs to external control through their interactions with them. GAFNA experienced vulnerability interdependence with CRS not only because CRS was its sole source of support, but because the nature of its relationship with CRS was not such that GAFNA had control over the allocation and use of resources provided. As a result, it was unable to respond to its community groups in a flexible manner.

GARDA is an example of a southern NGO that has received a combination of project-related support, which allows it to reach its community groups, and organizational development support, which sustains its operations. GARDA's overall sensitivity interdependence with northern NGOs has enabled it to interact with community groups in a relatively flexible and responsive way, rather than relegate its role to one of simply implementing northern NGOs' programmes. GARDA differs from ARD and OREINT in that the number and nature of its relationships with northern NGOs enhanced rather than hindered its relationships with community groups.

The case of GARDA proves instructive, since it was resource dependent and received resources from northern NGOs in the external environment, but was able to manage this interdependence in a way that did not result in GARDA being subject to external control. This suggests that there is nothing inherent in resource transfers from North to South which result in external control. Rather, it is the way in which the relationships are structured between northern and southern NGOs which creates such conditions. Overall, GARDA has learned how to acknowledge, assess and address the external environment whereas the other southern NGOs examined here have not.

There are several reasons for GARDA's success in managing its relationships with the external environment. First, GARDA had close ties with the village groups it works with. It has a charismatic leader, Kebba Bah, who is deeply rooted in his home community, where he has established the organization. Rather than relocate to the capital, Kebba Bah reinforced his local ties and influence by working with community groups in Soma and the surrounding area. The drawback of this approach is that some community groups have not dissociated Bah from the organization and will tell visitors that 'Kebba Bah helped us with this' rather than attribute the assistance to GARDA. GARDA also maintains a high profile at the field level by sending its staff to communities on a regular basis. This results in its easy and comfortable rapport with community groups. They discuss their concerns freely with GARDA, knowing that it will be as responsive as possible. The fact that they are not afraid to complain or raise issues with GARDA suggests that there is a certain level of trust.

This differs from the approach of ARD or OREINT in Sierra Leone, since these two southern NGOs are capital-city based, paying sporadic and infrequent visits to the groups with which they work. As a result, they have at times been perceived by some as a meddling presence or an unjustified intermediary looking for a share of resources, rather than as organizations which can help the community initiatives to thrive.

Because GARDA is so linked to its community groups, it has a clear understanding of what it can and cannot contribute to the development process. GARDA knows its comparative advantage. This enables it to say 'no' to donors or northern NGOs which offer it resources to carry out activities that either conflict with its aims or that it is not particularly well equipped to complete.

GARDA differs from most southern NGOs in The Gambia, which lack: a track record of designing activities and implementing projects; technical expertise; and established accounting, personnel, and inventory-control systems. Many southern NGOs in The Gambia were formed by one or two dynamic leaders who wanted to contribute to the community, especially their home community. As one NGO assessment (Sallah, 1994: B-5) concludes: 'Unlike the well-established NGOs, these newly formed organizations often lack vision. They are happy to adapt their program to fit the criteria of any and all funding schemes. Frequently this leads to problems as the NGO will claim it can do whatever you say you'll fund.'

If GARDA were to falter in its commitment to the community groups, its good relationships with its board of directors would keep it focused and accountable. This is markedly different from the other case study NGOs, and indeed from most southern NGOs. Many southern NGOs have boards in name only, or have no knowledge of the role that boards should play and the assistance they can give in terms of resource mobilization and strategic planning. GARDA utilizes its board to best advantage by having regular board meetings, ensuring that skilled professionals are on the board (not just high-profile individuals), and engaging in healthy debates regarding the organization's mission and direction.

Southern NGOs lack the resources they need to carry out their development programmes. They depend on northern NGOs to assist them by providing these resources. The number and nature of relationships that southern NGOs have with northern NGOs are key factors which should be considered in any analysis of southern NGOs' capacity. The case of ARD in Sierra Leone demonstrates the importance of the number of relationships, here so many that their transaction costs were a burden. By contrast, GAFNA had only one primary relationship with a northern NGO, and as a result was subject to vulnerability interdependence and external control.

This does not suggest that southern NGOs which have one relationship with a northern NGO are automatically vulnerable. The nature of that relationship may be such that the southern NGO is able to retain its integrity. Southern NGOs' dependence on northern NGOs is not problematic; but the unreliable nature of the latter's support is.

When southern NGOs do not know if support is forthcoming, they cannot plan activities, hire staff, or undertake programmes with grassroots groups. Northern NGOs' assistance to southern NGOs is often attached to programmes for grassroots groups, and as a result, southern NGOs are reduced to interacting with their beneficiary groups on the priorities, terms, and conditions established by northern NGOs. Southern NGOs by default become intermediary organizations carrying out northern NGOs' programmes. Because southern NGOs have limited (if any) input into northern NGOs' work, the former's comparative advantages and unique contributions to local development are undermined when they serve as operational arms of northern NGOs. In less extreme instances, southern NGOs become hybrid organizations that subsidize their own programmes through income earned working for northern NGOs.

Perhaps even more significant is the fact that southern NGOs' intermediary role transforms their relationships with grassroots groups from being an end in itself (that is something to be valued in its own right) to being a means to an end (that is a way of generating income). Overall, southern NGOs' relationships with northern NGOs are characterized by vulnerability interdependence, which subjects southern NGOs to external control, jeopardizing their contribution to a strong, association-based civil society.

7 Sustainable Idealism: Innovative Financing Strategies and NGOs' Contribution to Civil Society Development

The types of role that southern NGOs are expected to play in civil society necessitate autonomous organizations which are not beholden to external interests or swayed by pressures other than those which stem from their client groups. In fact, southern NGOs' responsiveness to donors rather than grassroots groups is the greatest threat to southern NGOs' ability to act as effective intermediaries, and to empower grassroots groups as part of civil society development.

This chapter suggests that in the light of their resource dependence, southern NGOs' contribution to civil society development needs to be reconsidered, and northern NGOs' capacity-building programmes reconfigured. Sustainable financing strategies are one area which should be prioritized in order to counter southern NGOs' resource dependence and to enable them to contribute to civil society development. The following sections consider each of these issues in turn.

Contribution to Civil Society

As the case studies of ARD, OREINT, and GAFNA demonstrated, northern NGOs' efforts to assist southern NGOs have often drawn these away from grassroots groups and redirected their focus towards the northern NGO providing support. ARD failed to establish close links with the more than 200 grassroots groups on its register and in effect operated as a consulting agency. OREINT had limited opportunities to engage with rural communities, and instead operated as an intermediary for northern NGOs.

GAFNA received a considerable influx of resources for its organizational development, but as an organization it was reshaped in the process, moving from an umbrella group of health and nutrition professionals to an implementing agency handling food aid for a bilateral donor and northern NGO. GAFNA has well-trained professional staff who could work with communities on the communities' terms, but they were unable to do so since GAFNA's time was taken up with the project that it implements for USAID and CRS. In this way, GAFNA is more responsive to CRS than to the grassroots groups with which it works.

If southern NGOs are to strengthen civil society in the course of their interactions with grassroots groups, then part of this process must entail either articulating interests on behalf of grassroots groups (at least in the short term) or, more appropriately, empowering grassroots groups to articulate their own interests. What role can compromised southern NGOs play in supporting civil society if, as Chazan (1992: 290) has said, 'associational autonomy is more central to the vitality of civil society than the availability of adequate means'?

While southern NGOs' contribution to civil society is predicated on their forming strong relationships with grassroots groups, it is equally important that they be able to disengage from these groups to avoid dependency. This issue is not a new one and many researchers (e.g. Desai, 1995) have examined southern NGOs' work with grassroots groups to determine appropriate organizational development strategies and time frames. What has not been examined in depth, or made explicit, is the need for grassroots groups to have the ability to 'exit' from relationships with southern NGOs if and when they prove unsatisfactory.

As in the case of ARD, OREINT, and GAFNA, grassroots groups had little or no choice as to which, if any, southern NGO acted as an intermediary between themselves and the northern NGOs. In all of these cases, northern NGOs approached the southern and contracted their services to work with grassroots groups. When these groups did approach ARD or OREINT, for example, these southern NGOs lacked the

resources necessary to engage the grassroots groups meaningfully on their own terms.

Exit, Voice, and Loyalty

The dynamic between southern NGOs and grassroots groups
as it relates to civil society development can be analysed using
Hirschman's (1970) concepts of 'exit, voice, and loyalty'. In
short, strengthening civil society entails strengthening the
'exit' option for grassroots groups. This includes the opportunity to exit from state-provided services or southern NGO
programmes when they prove inadequate. Competition
between service providers and a plurality of associational
forms affords grassroots groups the opportunity to be selective
in forming relationships with southern NGOs. And, in the
cases where northern NGOs contract southern NGOs to provide services to the grassroots groups, a group should at least
have the potential to request the services of a different southern NGO where there is one.

Where the exit option does not exist – and in so many rural
areas it does not, given the absence of state services or capable
southern NGOs with access to resources – grassroots groups
have the 'voice' option. This is a residual category which in a
sense can be equated with interest articulation. Grassroots
groups can use their voices to let northern and southern NGOs
know what it is they like or dislike about the southern NGO
which provides them with services. This voice will help to
increase grassroots groups' commitment to development
efforts, and ensure their sustainability as a result. Salmen
(1987; 1992: 14) has observed that the poor are more likely to
invest resources or labour in an organization's work if they
have a voice in what it is doing.

'Loyalty' is the final factor which figures in Hirschman's
schema, and this makes exit less likely while at the same time
giving scope to voice. Southern NGOs need to create loyalty
among the grassroots groups with which they work. Where
there is loyalty, the likelihood of voice increases and the desire
for exit decreases, since people have an attachment which
prompts them to express their concerns rather than exit altogether. Only those southern NGOs which retain relationships

with grassroots groups in the face of these groups' exit option can claim to contribute truly to civil society development. Capacity-enhancing initiatives that simply assist southern NGOs without enhancing their ability to make grassroots groups' voice heard, and to respond to that voice, do nothing for civil society development.

If southern NGOs want to gain grassroots groups' loyalty, they will need to change the ways in which they operate in order to demonstrate their responsiveness to these groups. This will make exit by these groups less likely. Southern NGOs, however, can make these changes only if they have the latitude in their relationships with northern NGOs to allow them to do so. Relationships characterized by vulnerability interdependence do not provide this latitude. In order to contribute to civil society development, capacity-building programmes must increase southern NGOs' ability to provide services to grassroots groups in ways which increase these groups' loyalty and voice and, as a result, decrease their desire for exit.

Not all southern NGOs have empowerment of grassroots groups as their overriding concern. Many southern NGOs have been formed under the pretext of assisting grassroots groups, but in actual fact are motivated by the promise of outside resources. The capacity of these southern NGOs should not be developed. Rather, only those which demonstrate commitment to the empowerment of grassroots groups should be supported.

Southern NGOs' Comparative Advantage

Southern NGOs need to be clear about their comparative advantage in assisting grassroots groups. This will strengthen their bargaining position *vis-à-vis* the northern NGOs with which they interact, while at the same time ensuring southern NGOs' autonomy and integrity to their own agendas.

As secondary functions to assisting grassroots groups, southern NGOs' contribution with respect to civil society development might include the following.

1   Southern NGOs have an ability to provide employment

opportunities, particularly for displaced, educated, middle-class professionals. This may ease the burden of structural adjustment programmes in which civil servants are made redundant. These opportunities for skilled employment are particularly useful in the absence of higher education posts or business/industry positions. In addition, southern NGOs may serve as a training ground for future civil servants. This decreases the likelihood of 'brain drain', by which educated classes with political and economic interests move abroad. Increased employment opportunities for middle-class professionals, and the development of this socio-economic stratum, help to create a politically and economically active class willing to protect its interests.

In Chile, by 1990 there were 300–400 NGOs which had sprung up in response to the military regime's repressive policies and its efforts to reduce the public-sector role. This provided employment and income for the displaced professionals and political opponents of the regime. In Latin America and the Caribbean generally, the Inter-American Foundation identified 11,000 NGOs. Many of these are, however, in the words of Bebbington and Farrington (1993: 202), 'non-politicized yuppie NGOs ... rooted in the economic displacement of middle class professionals from both public and private sectors'.

In Brazil, a recent survey of NGO activity (Fernandes and Carneiro, 1995) revealed that 85 per cent of NGO leaders had college diplomas and 39 per cent had graduate degrees. Many of these leaders received their education abroad, an opportunity not available to the majority of the population. But this level of education and privilege did not necessarily distance them from their causes. The same study found that during the repression of the 1960s and early 1970s, of the sample of NGO leaders surveyed two had their citizens' rights suspended, 11 were taken to court, six were fired from their jobs, 17 were imprisoned, seven were tortured, six were exiled, and seven chose voluntary exile.

2   Southern NGOs have an ability to utilize and cultivate informal skills and local knowledge which are in abundance in developing countries, but often undervalued. Southern NGOs can animate people to value their own knowledge and to use it to order their own realities, particularly as they search for solutions to development problems. This transformative approach to civil society development relies on the beneficiaries of development assistance shaping the decisions which affect them (Gaventa, 1995).

3   Southern NGOs have an ability to create and maintain local networks of grassroots groups, resource people, and traditional leaders. Southern NGOs' knowledge of the socio-cultural conditions of the countries in which they operate uniquely positions them to interact with the grassroots groups that they are designed to assist, and to identify key people who may be able to influence the wider processes which affect development outcomes.

4   Southern NGOs have an ability to increase advocacy skills and to create in the process constituencies for reform, through the provision of culturally appropriate and context-specific training and mobilization.

5   Southern NGOs have an ability to foster national identity by taking a lead role in development processes; a role traditionally undertaken by outside agents (such as religious groups, northern NGOs, donors). For example, in Kazakhstan, where two centuries of foreign domination followed fragmented, clan-based nomadism, NGOs may foster a Kazakh national identity through their activities to revive and promote the Kazakh language, restore traditional names to cities and landmarks, and revise history lessons to reflect a Kazakh national perspective. In South Africa, where racial identities have split the nation, NGOs can foster cooperation and understanding through development programmes. World Vision has undertaken sponsorship and development education programmes aimed at uniting the various ethnic communities.

Northern NGOs should work with southern NGOs on the basis of the latter's identified comparative advantage. However, it is more likely that northern NGOs work with southern NGOs on a less strategic basis. Northern NGOs often learn of southern NGOs through development networks or from southern NGOs sending them project proposals, rather than as a result of an institutional assessment of all the key southern NGOs working in a country. Most significantly, northern NGOs may contract southern NGOs to work with grassroots groups without realizing that southern NGOs' relationships with these groups are weak or even non-existent. Northern NGOs may engage with southern NGOs without realizing which others exist, or what specifically one southern NGO can offer which is different from others. As a result, northern and southern NGOs engaged in capacity-building initiatives tend to be ill-matched from the beginning and without the mutual interests which would ensure continued exchanges.

Capacity Building Reconfigured

Once southern NGOs are clear about their comparative advantages, they can begin to market themselves more effectively to external actors, without the fear of losing their organizational identity by engaging in activities which fall outside their stated agenda. There may not be an ideal type of southern NGO that capacity enhancing should aim to develop, but characteristics of capacity-enhancing initiatives which would enable southern NGOs to consolidate their links with grassroots groups and contribute to civil society include:

- being designed in consultation with constituent groups;
- providing project assistance for grassroots groups as well as organizational development support for southern NGOs;
- offering at least some untied aid to southern NGOs to enable them to respond to grassroots groups' needs;
- being evaluated by grassroots groups against their own criteria for success, negotiated at the beginning of the project, to ensure that southern NGOs' work contributes

to political and economic empowerment of grassroots groups.

Capacity-enhancing initiatives must have at their core an understanding of whose interests, whose goals, and whose preferences are to prevail in organizations. Currently, capacity enhancing for southern NGOs tends to amplify northern NGOs' needs while suppressing those of grassroots groups. If organizational structures as well as functions are shaped by the outcomes of conflicts between various actors, then because northern NGOs are generally more powerful and better resourced than grassroots groups, southern NGOs' structures and functions are more likely to reflect northern NGOs' priorities and preferences than those of the groups. This jeopardizes not only southern NGOs' ability to deliver basic services to these groups, but also these NGOs' capacity to strengthen civil society in the process.

Northern NGOs could incorporate the following strategies into capacity-enhancing initiatives in order to improve southern NGOs' effectiveness and ability to acknowledge, assess, and address the external environment.

1   Northern NGOs could modify the training they provide for southern NGOs' managers to improve their abilities to carry out what Pfeffer and Salancik (1978) refer to as the 'symbolic role of management'. In the symbolic role, 'The manager is a symbol of the organization and its success or failure, a scapegoat, and a symbol of personal or individual control over social actions and outcomes' (Pfeffer and Salancik, 1978: 263).

What is important about this role is that the symbolic leader serves as a figurehead, and reassures the various stakeholders of the organization that someone is in charge and can control organizational activities and fortunes. While the reality of the organization may be far more complex, this reassurance is often all that is needed to boost internal organizational morale, or to present a positive public image in times of trouble. A strong, symbolic leader is essential to fundraising, since this person can generate confidence in and enthusiasm about the organization's work. Pfeffer and Salancik

(1978: 263) contend that 'The symbol of control and personal causation provides the prospect of stability for the social system.'

The symbolic leader is important to the organization whether or not the manager actually accounts for variance in organizational results. When problems emerge within NGOs, organizations can solve them by removing the manager, since the failures will have largely been attributed to that person. In a sense, this deflects the blame away from an NGO and gives it an opportunity to reorganize its own operations and activities. By changing the symbolic leader, NGOs can respond to external pressures emanating from their environments without losing a significant amount of discretion over their activities and structure.

It is important to recognize, however, that leaders are not only symbols. This is one of the three critical roles they can play. The other two are the 'responsive role' and the 'discretionary role'. In the responsive role, the manager serves as a processor and responder to the demands and constraints coming from the environment. In the discretionary role, the manager is responsible for altering the system of constraints and dependencies confronting the NGO. This role entails serving as a focal point for the organization's success and failures. In effect, the manager is seen as the personification of the organization, its activities, and its outcomes. The manager becomes the target for external publics who want to vent their pleasure or displeasure with the organization's actions or performance. Managers may either adapt activities to the constraints imposed by interdependence with the environment or alter constraints by attempting to change the environment itself.

2   Northern NGOs could facilitate southern NGOs' diversification of their funding base by providing training in fundraising and public relations. Staff exchanges between northern and southern NGOs may prove especially beneficial in this area, since southern NGOs could learn from northern NGOs' technical skills and media knowledge, while northern NGOs could learn from

southern NGOs about development issues, and thus present them more accurately to donors.

3   Northern NGOs could promote development education so that the public is more inclined to support both official and private contributions to development efforts, particularly those which allow beneficiaries greater control in the allocation and use of funds. Development education is essential to challenge many people's ignorance regarding the source of development problems, and to encourage people to support overseas aid, particularly amidst the current funding cuts in governmental assistance. Structural changes brought on by lobbying and advocacy in the North may ease the constraints southern NGOs face in their broader external environments.

4   Northern NGOs could strengthen southern NGOs' boards of advisors by helping them to institute and standardize procedures, practices, and guidelines for board members. Board functions include determining policy, implementing selected policies, monitoring policies, and providing advice and consent on activities. There are two types of board: a governing board whose function is to control and assist the organization; and an advisory board whose function is to provide assistance rather than make policy decisions. Regardless of the type of board southern NGOs have, strong boards would enable them to remain accountable to their donors while preserving their integrity in carrying out their work with beneficiary groups (Heimovics, Herman, and Coughlin, 1993). Boards facilitate southern NGOs' assessment of their comparative advantages and their strategic interaction with actors in the external environment. They decrease these NGOs' vulnerability to external control by anchoring the organizations and guarding against co-optation.

   Strengthening boards of advisors can equip national NGOs to assess their organizational environment, so that they remain loyal to their own identities as they seek increased assistance from the external environment, or adopt financing strategies which result in a rapid influx of funding. Boards help NGOs to balance client satisfaction with the ability to attract funding. Generally, the board's functions include (Conrad and Glenn, 1983: 92):

- determining policy;
- implementing selected policies;
- monitoring policy implementation;
- offering advice and consent.

Overall, the board can offer the following benefits to the NGO (Conrad and Glenn, 1983: 116):

- expertise in technical areas for which the NGO could not pay;
- sanction of various external publics;
- knowledge of various facts about the community;
- continuity of policy and programme;
- ability to serve as a spokesperson;
- influence to attract financial, human, and public resources;
- preservation of internal democracy;
- capacity for critical review of operations;
- ability to affect changes in the organization;
- collective wisdom.

Many NGOs have boards that reflect little or no input from people outside the NGO community, and as a result lack the sharpness or critical perspective that would allow them to move towards their stated goals. Many board members, and boards as a whole, are unclear or unaware of their roles and responsibilities *vis-à-vis* the agencies themselves or their legal obligations. Some boards become so intimately involved in the daily operations of the agencies that they usurp the role of the executive directors, while others are so uninvolved that they have no knowledge of what goes on. One particularly interesting mechanism for increasing boards' capacity and ability to function effectively is to have reciprocal board placements, or board members from southern NGOs elected to the boards of northern NGOs. The International Institute for Environment and Development, CUSO, the World Wide Fund for Nature, and World Vision have successfully implemented these strategies for years. NOVIB sponsors a 'Guest at Your Table' programme, which is primarily a joint fundraising effort by which southern NGOs meet donor groups in The Netherlands, and contribute material for newsletters.

5   Northern NGOs could finance the position of grants compliance officer, charged with the task of acquiring resources and reporting on their use. This would decrease southern NGOs' transaction costs with other actors and enable them to manage their interdependence. It would also free managers and project staff from these responsibilities, which means they could concentrate on roles they are better equipped to fill. SCF/USA has used this approach to manage the number of relationships that it has with donors. If southern NGOs had similar positions, possibly funded by northern NGOs in the context of capacity building, the field staff would be freer to carry out their respective roles rather than being bogged down by administrative duties. This would ensure that additional external financing does not distance southern NGOs from the beneficiaries whom they were established to serve.

6   Northern NGOs could adopt creative financing strategies when working with southern NGOs. Examples of these include consortium funding, endowments, and the provision of structures like office buildings which could save on overhead costs and potentially generate income. The case studies of southern NGOs in Sierra Leone and The Gambia revealed that multiple accountabilities, reporting formats, and banking requirements hindered southern NGOs' capacity to manage all the multiple linkages with actors in the external environment necessary to obtain resources. In addition to

requiring more user-friendly administrative procedures, southern NGOs could benefit from the decreased
transaction costs associated with obtaining resources
from fewer donors in the external environment. The
following section explores these strategies in greater
detail.

Sustainable Financing Strategies

Different people have different things in mind when they
speak of 'financial sustainability'. For some it means that
NGOs can manage on their own without donor support. For
others, it means that they manage the funds that they do have
so well that donors continue to support them. And for others,
it means that NGOs have invested the funds that they do
receive so that they can live off the investment earnings later.

Specific illustrative attempts that NGOs around the world
have made to acquire resources and to manage them effectively are discussed here, in order to suggest possible options
which might enable NGOs to have greater autonomy over
their programmes, and therefore more organizational integrity. This will strengthen their link with grassroots groups, and
as a result their ability to contribute to civil society development. These strategies are:

- soliciting philanthropic contributions;
- engaging with the corporate sector;
- hosting special events;
- using returnable loans.

Soliciting Philanthropic Contributions

Soliciting philanthropic contributions has been a new direction
which many Latin American NGOs have attempted. This is not
without reason. According to estimates, the largest block of
available investment capital in the world, approximately
US$350 billion, is held by wealthy Latin Americans in Swiss
and US accounts. In a 1994 cover story in *Forbes* magazine
entitled 'Wealth comes to Latin America: the world's 291

billionaires', Latin America had the highest number of billionaires entering the list, suggesting that there is more potential
for philanthropic support there than in any other region of the
world. In addition to gaining contributions from the ultra-rich,
NGOs have benefited from assistance derived from the middle
classes.

Tapping into philanthropic contributions will probably be
very difficult for NGOs in new democracies for several reasons. The first has been mentioned before: the legislative and
tax structures in new democracies are not equipped to encourage private giving or facilitate NGOs' acceptance of such
donations. Secondly, the economy in new democracies is
usually marked by a decline in the middle classes and a
widening gap between the haves and the have nots. In order to
raise money successfully in Central Asia, for example, NGOs
would need to draw on the wealth generated by the 5 per cent
of the population who are benefiting from the transition.
Finally, new democracies are often characterized by low levels
of confidence in government, which may mean that money is
stored outside a country rather than reinvested inside. According to the Inter-American Foundation (Thompson, 1995: 52),
'Economic stability and the basic conditions for generating
genuine wealth seem to be prerequisites for mobilizing significant local resources for development.'

Engaging with the Corporate Sector

Perhaps a more likely new direction for NGOs in new democracies to adopt, at least in the first instance, is engaging with
the corporate sector or even state-owned businesses. In Venezuela, community groups have received funding from the
state-owned oil company Petroleos de Venezuela (PDVSA),
the second largest in the world. PDVSA entered into a legal
cooperative agreement with the Inter-American Foundation in
order to co-fund grassroots initiatives in employment and
income generation, agricultural production, alternative education and occupational training for youth, community organ-
izing, and democratic participation.

UK NGOs like Oxfam, SCF, Help the Aged, and Amnesty
International have linked up with the Co-operative Bank in a

scheme to provide 'affinity cards', which operate like any standard credit card except that the Bank donates a portion of the proceeds to the NGOs. For example, for each customer who obtains a card, the Bank donates approximately US$8.00 to the NGO nominated. The bank will also donate a further US$0.40 or so every time the customer spends US$150.00. One NGO which has been linked to the scheme has received approximately US$350 million since the card was introduced in 1989.

Other NGOs have allied themselves with showbusiness in order to reap a percentage of returns from movie premières. The Prince's Trust, the NGO affiliated with Prince Charles, earned approximately US$400,000 following the 1995 première of the James Bond film *Goldeneye*. Projected returns from the première of *Star Wars* made the Prince's Trust approximately US$300,000 richer. The 4,000 guests who paid to attend the London première of *101 Dalmations* in the Royal Albert Hall helped to raise money for three different charities. An estimated nine out of 10 film premières are now associated with a charitable cause. Other British charities hope to raise at least US$800,000 through fundraising hikes and bike rides, which allow people to have a vacation while easing their social conscience. Oxfam UK has booked 50 people on such a trip and each one will raise about US$2,000 for Oxfam after all expenses have been met. In addition to the US$100,000 that Oxfam hopes to clear, it has the added benefit of working in the areas the supporters are visiting, so that it can show them what it is doing in the field, and where the proceeds from the fundraising will be directed.

While most national NGOs will not have the resources or skills necessary to broker such arrangements, there are lessons to be learned from these experiences of building relationships intra- and inter-sectorally. The first is the three-dimensional perspective gained by collaboration between the state, the private sector, and NGOs. This increases the potential to develop innovative solutions to development problems. Second, it provides an opportunity for organizations to pool financial and technical resources and deliver them to community groups, which in turn can increase the scale and scope of their activities.

The Body Shop aims to support local communities and

NGOs through its Community Trade programme. Suppliers are identified from socially and economically marginalized groups around the world. These relationships benefit the Body Shop, since it gains access to unique products and can assure its customers that no people or places have been exploited in the process of producing or acquiring the goods that it sells. Suppliers gain training and information, which enable them to market their wares successfully. While this trade with communities is currently only a small part of the Body Shop's overall operations, it is committed to increasing this practice. And because not all businesses are openly concerned with social and ethical practices, this model may not be readily replicable elsewhere. It would be possible, however, to create pilot projects based on the Body Shop's work.

Hosting Special Events

One strategy which does offer a lot of promise for NGOs' ability to address their external environment is hosting special events. The Instituto Dominicano de Desarrollo Integral (IDDI) is one NGO that has used sporting events to raise funds. In fact, between 1992 and 1995 IDDI raised US$115,110 by organizing special events, while it received only US$94,800 in corporate donations and US$84,690 from individual donations. By encouraging famous professional baseball players (originating from the Dominican Republic) to contribute their names and money to fundraising campaigns, the IDDI raised money by selling autographed memorabilia. It used the same celebrities to organize golf tournaments, in which baseball players who were amateur golfers teed up alongside wealthy people in the Dominican Republic who would pay for the privilege of golfing with the stars. Airlines and golf resorts also donated services, which resulted in free publicity for them. These events served the dual purpose of encouraging a local culture of philanthropic giving, and strengthening civil society, since communities worked to develop themselves.

In the UK, the St Thomas Fund for the Homeless has recently undertaken a 'Diminishing Dinner Party' as a means of fundraising for the NGO. One couple invites five other couples to dinner for a charge of about US$10 per couple, excluding the host couple. This is donated to the St Thomas Fund. Each initial guest couple invites five further couples to a subsequent dinner party, and each of these five guest couples invites four more couples to a party, and so on. At each party, an information leaflet is given to each couple. The list below summarizes how the money (in US$)is raised:

- each of the 5 invites 5 couples   = 25 couples @ $10 = $250;
- each of the 25 invites 4 couples   = 100 couples @ $10 = $1,000;
- each of the 100 invites 3 couples = 300 couples @ $10 = $3,000;
- each of the 300 invites 2 couples = 600 couples @ $10 = $6,000;
- each of the 600 invites 1 couple   = 600 couples @ $10 = $6,000;
- plus $50 from the initial dinner party = $16,300.

Not only is this a lucrative fundraiser for the NGO, but it provides an opportunity to mobilize the community, and to make the public more aware about issues of homelessness and addiction to drugs and alcohol, which often results in homelessness.

Using Returnable Loans

Finally, NGOs can address the external environment by engaging in productive borrowing, where the expected return from borrowed funds exceeds the cost of borrowing. Charities Aid Foundation (CAF) in the UK has recently established a Returnable Donations scheme which NGOs can use to finance new projects, which in turn attracts further funds. CAF hopes to implement the programme in Eastern Europe in the near future. Donors make Returnable Donations to the Social Investment Fund for a period of six months, one, two, three or five years, or some other agreed period. Outright gifts are also accepted. The Fund then makes loans at rates lower than bank terms. As loans are repaid or guarantees expire, the money in the Fund can be recycled to benefit further projects.

By adopting and supporting innovative financing methods, northern NGOs and donors could increase southern NGOs' capacity manifold, and facilitate their contributions to civil society. Funding of innovative mechanisms like endowments, trusts, and foundations, or the establishment of donor consortia to fund NGO activities jointly, are precluded by either procurement policies or the difficulty of adhering to strict accounting and reporting requirements imposed by central governments. Other limitations which are particularly relevant to weaker, newer NGOs include the following (Davies, 1996: 12):

> The process of negotiating agreement may lead to a format that expresses the highest common denominator, increasing the overall scale of the information demands on the funded NGO. While this is likely to be seen as a negative change by the funded NGO it may not necessarily be so from the point of view of beneficiaries;
>   If all donor NGOs are receiving the same information from the funded NGO then what is the unique value that they as funders are providing?;
>   The funded NGO loses 'room to manoeuvre' where it could tailor its reports to each donor's individual needs and biases. Because mechanisms like these have not been widely adopted, southern NGOs have not achieved the autonomy they need from donors and northern NGOs, and have been used as service delivery instruments in the achievement of donor objectives.

In spite of the constraints northern NGOs and donors face implementing consortia funding, endowments, and trusts and foundations, some examples of how these approaches have been put into practice are discussed here. These innovative mechanisms could help NGOs to move away from the project cycle and towards financial sustainability, by which core costs are covered and an organization can exercise discretion over its agenda.

The Sarvodaya Shramadana Movement in Sri Lanka was funded by a donor consortium with a view to improving long-term planning, gaining access to a committed three-year budget, receiving better remuneration for workers and improvement of their skills, and adopting a single comprehensive monitoring, evaluation, and reporting system for all donors. However, the NGO found that there was little dialogue at consortium meetings and that donor representatives acted as executors of decisions already made at headquarters. The formation of the consortium increased rather than decreased Sarvodaya's workload, particularly that of the headquarters' staff, who had to deal with the numerous evaluators, monitors, and experts who visited the NGO. Overall, the top-down nature of the consortium contradicted Sarvodaya's primary aim of fostering participatory democracy and developing an organizational structure which would facilitate this.

USAID has incorporated endowments into its work in Latin America and the Caribbean since the mid-1980s. In April 1996, USAID Administrator J. Brian Atwood requested a study on the experiences of USAID and other donors in setting up endowments and foundations. The study (USAID, 1996: 1) concluded that:

> Under the appropriate conditions, endowments can be a viable option for providing long-term sustainable development in countries with or without a USAID presence;
>
> Using endowments can be an important strategy for increasing the capabilities of indigenous organizations as development partners;
>
> Strong institutions that are well-managed and have successful track records are an essential prerequisite to funding an endowment;
>
> By their very nature, endowments involve less USAID monitoring and oversight than other types of activities. Instead safeguards are built into the endowment design.

In addition, the country's legal, regulatory, and financial environment needs to be amenable to establishing an endowment. This may limit the success of this approach in new democracies where the legal enabling environment has yet to be put in place.

Another related approach is creating foundation-like organizations (FLOs) which can serve as intermediaries for ODA support to civil society in the South. The US-based Synergos Institute and the Inter-American Foundation have recently incorporated this approach to their work with southern NGOs. Synergos has found in the course of evaluating its work (Tomlinson, 1996: 244) that FLOs play a major role in fostering and funding civil society's contributions to development throughout the South. FLOs take many forms, but the majority of them combine support, advocacy, and programme elements with grant-making and the stimulation of local philanthropy. They have served as effective intermediaries for domestic civil society groups and government, donors, and the private sector. This allows them to tap diverse sources of income for NGO projects, and to serve as a channel for northern funding agencies or even southern governments.

Finally, timing may be everything in adopting capacity-building programmes with southern NGOs. Avina (1993: 453) has described what he calls the 'NGO life cycle' and maintains that 'Being able to recognize the characteristic descriptive elements of the different phases of organizational development better positions one to understand the nature of an NGO's relationship with donors, beneficiaries and the world around it.'

The stages in the cycle are: start-up; expansion; consolidation; and close-down. Most NGOs in new democracies are struggling with the first stage of starting up their activities, and few have been able to acquire the resources necessary to expand them. When they have, they have often done so according to donors' plans and priorities. What southern NGOs require is the capacity-building assistance that will allow them to adopt creative financing strategies such as those described above in order to manage the consolidation of their organizations. If northern NGOs and donors are aware of the NGOs' level of development, they can structure their programmes accordingly. The adoption of innovative financing strategies needs to be linked to the NGO life cycle. For example, early stages of NGO development require an organization to mobilize resources, while latter stages require it to capitalize its operations.

Southern NGOs' fundraising strategies may contribute to the development of a local philanthropic culture, and encourage citizen participation at all levels. If southern NGOs are able to garner resources from the external environment effectively, and manage their existing resources strategically, then they will be more likely to engage with grassroots groups in ways which strengthen the groups' position in civil society and their contribution to it. Southern NGOs' contribution to democratic and sustainable development rests on their ability to acquire resources in ways which enhance rather than hinder their relationships with grassroots groups.

Areas for Further Study

Changing northern NGOs' capacity-building relationships with southern NGOs is a necessary but not sufficient precondition to increasing southern NGOs' capacity and ability to contribute to civil society. There are other important factors that affect southern NGOs' relationships with grassroots groups which could be considered in future research. Most importantly, the link between southern NGOs and grassroots groups needs to be explored in more depth to determine the extent to which it exists in the first place, and to assess the ways in which these groups are able to avoid reliance on southern NGOs in the long term. One of the practical ways that this might be implemented is by engaging grassroots groups in participatory assessments of southern NGOs' activities.

The second area which needs further exploration is the way the relationship between northern and southern NGOs relates to other variables that affect the latter's capacity. The southern NGOs' ability to raise local resources is one important variable to be considered. Another is the nature of the political regime in power and southern NGOs' relationship with it. Where governments are supportive of southern NGOs' operations, they may have increased room to manoeuvre, and influence in the policy-making process. Where there is tension and competition for resources between southern NGOs and governments, southern NGOs' ability to work with grassroots groups and to engage in policy dialogue is limited. Southern NGOs in Latin America offer interesting examples of how collaboration with governments, particularly at the municipal level, can yield positive results (Reilly, 1995). Another factor which affects southern NGOs' capacity is the existence of clear and supportive regulatory environments and tax structures. The former give southern NGOs legitimate space in which to operate, while the latter enable them to raise funds and to accept charitable donations.

It is clear that the way in which northern NGOs relate to southern NGOs affects the latter's capacity. Further exploration is needed to understand the extent to which northern NGOs' relationships with southern NGOs affects the latter's relationships with grassroots groups. Wellard and Copestake (1993) provide a good starting point for this debate in their examination of southern NGOs' effectiveness in strengthening grassroots groups and local organizations. It is possible that southern NGOs will replicate patterns of relationships that they have with northern NGOs in their work with these groups. This may result in these groups' vulnerability interdependence with southern NGOs. If that is the case then clearly southern NGOs will be undermining rather than enhancing civil society.

In fact, where southern NGOs do not empower grassroots groups, or where they bypass government structures, they may actually have an adverse effect on civil society development. A study of the NGO sector in Bolivia (Arellano-Lopez and Petras, 1994) found that strengthening NGOs has coincided with the weakening of state agencies and grassroots groups and, perhaps more importantly, undermined the ability of Latin American countries to develop alternative development agendas to those supported by the international financial community, and the ability of opposition groups to call for such alternatives.

Enhancing the capacity of southern NGOs does not mean creating independent, autonomous organizations. Such entities do not exist. Instead, capacity enhancing entails critical reflection on the part of northern NGOs to discern what is their most appropriate role *vis-à-vis* southern NGOs and how best to carry it out, particularly in the face of constricting donor conditions. Useful capacity-enhancing initiatives must focus on assisting southern NGOs in their efforts to acquire resources without compromising their integrity, and to interact with the environment in ways that ensure southern NGOs' organizational survival. More importantly, these initiatives must enable southern NGOs to reach groups at the grassroots level and, in the process, contribute to the development of a strong, association-based civil society.

Sustainable financing strategies are promising, but are not a panacea for southern NGOs' development. Relationships between northern and southern NGOs are conditioned by power, control, resources, and accountability – all essential areas to address if southern NGOs are to realize their potential. Sustainable financing strategies offer some hope of southern NGOs gaining more power over resources, control over how they are used, and therefore accountability for their use.

Making these changes is essential if southern NGOs are to play any meaningful role in development.

With the appropriate capacity-building assistance, southern NGOs can link state and society together to make the state more responsive and therefore legitimate. Southern NGOs can also mediate between the state and grassroots groups to ensure that policies are adjusted to reflect these groups' interests. Finally, southern NGOs can assist economic development by providing basic services to meet people's needs, especially when the market and state have failed to do so (Barkan, McNulty, and Ayeni, 1991). Southern NGOs' survival is primarily important only to the extent that they serve grassroots groups, since this, rather than an intermediary tier, is the level upon which civil society development must be predicated. As Brown and Korten (1991: 78) say, 'the distinctive role of NGOs comes in strengthening civil society and people's capacity to participate'. Democracy by proxy is neither sustainable nor desirable.

8 Conclusions: 'Just Say No': Strengthening Southern NGOs' Capacity to Contribute to Civil Society

Sustainable financing strategies like those described in the previous chapter are essential to southern NGOs' capacity and ability to contribute to civil society development. These strategies ensure that southern NGOs are linked to the client groups which they were established to assist; therefore, they enable southern NGOs to counter their resource dependence and vulnerability to external control. Sustainable financing strategies encourage southern NGOs to integrate into the economies in which they exist, rather than rely on often unreliable donor financing. When southern NGOs have command over even a portion of the resources they need to survive, they are better placed to respond to beneficiaries' needs.

Innovative financing strategies, however, are not a panacea. Southern NGOs find disincentives to linking with businesses, or adopting business-like strategies to raise capital. The political ties of some businesses taint the NGOs that take funding from them. There are also dangers that NGOs will unwittingly receive 'dirty money' from businesses: money from a business which has aims inimical to an NGO's. Overall, the country's legal and tax structures may not enable southern NGOs to collaborate with businesses. For example, tax law may not allow businesses to receive deductions for their support of non-profit organizations, or NGOs may find it difficult to register as non-profits in order to take advantage of that status. These issues have become so important that the British Institute of Charity Fundraising Managers has issued guidelines which will help to steer NGOs legally and ethically through these murky waters.

Ultimately, if southern NGOs are to realize their comparative advantage in the development process they require greater capacity to acknowledge, assess, and address the external environment. They need to understand the important role that the external environment plays in their operations; they need to be aware of which organizations or businesses can provide them with resources; and they need to know how to acquire resources from those organizations or businesses. If northern NGOs and donors redesigned capacity-building interventions to include these skills, rather than simply those related to the internal functioning of southern NGOs, they would enhance the latter's prospects of sustainability and autonomy. This has implications for their ability to contribute to civil society development, since an organization which is compromised in the process of seeking funds and beholden to outside interests cannot articulate the needs of the clients that it serves.

One of the greatest indicators of a southern NGO's ability to acknowledge, assess, and address the external environment is its readiness to say 'no' to funding opportunities which conflict with its mission or its beneficiaries' priorities. If southern NGOs take a firm stand with respect to what assistance they will receive from northern NGOs, and the role they will play in the development process, they will gradually be able to shift the power paradigm to give the beneficiaries of development interventions a greater say in their identification, design, and implementation. It is only when southern NGOs empower grassroots groups, or give voice to their needs, that these NGOs can contribute meaningfully to civil society development.

Too often, southern NGOs which are intermediaries for northern NGOs have been proxy for the beneficiaries they were designed to serve. While this may not be desirable, it has been at times unavoidable given the geographic and cultural differences between these groups and the donors who support them. Southern NGOs can provide a useful linking function when they are solidly grounded in their relationships with these groups. But they cannot take the place of these groups, as has often been the case. For example, some southern NGOs, rather than their clients, have a seat at the table in negotiations with international organizations like the United Nations and the World Bank. Southern NGOs receive enormous amounts of capacity-building assistance, given their presumed comparative advantage in reaching client groups, particularly the poor and marginalized. The way in which this support is channelled, however, compromises southern NGOs' ability to respond flexibly to these groups, empower them to articulate their needs, or give voice to their needs. The disproportionate emphasis on southern NGOs rather than beneficiaries has skewed civil society development strategies. Rather than contributing to the consolidation of democracy, southern NGOs have largely created democracy by proxy. If northern NGOs and donors are serious about their commitment to civil society development, and expenditures in this area suggest that they are, then they need to redress this imbalance.

The politics of North–South NGO relationships informs southern NGOs' relationships with beneficiaries, and so strengthening the latter must begin by reconstructing the former. Northern NGOs need to decrease the uncertainty around their provision of resources to southern NGOs, and refocus their attention from the internal variables to the external variables constraining organizational capacity. The framework of inter-organizational influence offers a tool for assessing inequalities in exchange relationships, and for unveiling the often hidden sources of power that the weaker actor has with respect to the stronger one. And recognizing that northern NGOs subject southern NGOs to external control through relationships characterized by vulnerability interdependence is the first step to changing this.

There is a growing urgency to redress these imbalances. Northern and southern NGOs increasingly receive funds from official government sources, and therefore they have come under greater scrutiny and pressure to account for their activities. And as southern NGOs receive a larger proportion of official development assistance, they are viewed by some governments as competitors, particularly when they by-pass government development programmes or use their influx of resources to engage in advocacy or lobbying activities.

Such instances underline the political nature of NGOs' work, and of their relationships with one another, with governments and with client groups. NGOs' relationships are conditioned by power dynamics, since northern NGOs tend to have resources which southern NGOs need for development activities. This renders southern NGOs vulnerable to northern, and creates a power paradigm in which northern NGOs are able to exercise control over southern. NGOs' relationships with the state are fraught with difficulty, since their presence potentially alters the political landscape, as NGOs empower groups to make claims on government and demand increased and better access to public services. Finally, NGOs' relationships with their client groups are political, since NGOs' role is to support development. Development is about change and change is inherently political.

NGOs, particularly southern NGOs, have moved from the role of bit player on the development stage to one which commands the spotlight. Unless they are able to counter their resource dependence and vulnerability to external control, they will fail to win over their audiences, most importantly their client groups. If they are successful, and if northern NGOs make the changes in their own operations and capacity-building programmes which will allow them to be so, then southern NGOs can make a meaningful contribution to the development drama.

References

Agbaje, A. (1990). 'In Search of Building Blocks: The State, Civil Society, Voluntary Action and Grassroots Development in Africa.' *Africa Quarterly* **30**(3–4): 24–40.

Anderson, L. (1998). 'Relentless Campaigns of Hollow Promises.' *Chicago Tribune* 15 March.

Arellano-Lopez, S. and Petras, J. (1994). 'NGOs and Poverty Alleviation in Bolivia.' *Development and Change* **25**(3): 555–68.

Avina, J. (1993). 'The Evolutionary Life Cycles of Non-Governmental Development Organizations.' *Public Administration and Development* **13**: 453–74.

Baldwin, D. (1989). *Paradoxes of Power*. Oxford: Basil Blackwell.

Barkan, J., McNulty, M., and Ayeni, M. (1991). '"Hometown" Voluntary Associations, Local Development, and the Emergence of Civil Society in Western Nigeria.' *Journal of Modern African Studies* **29**(3): 457–80.

Bebbington, A. and Farrington, J. (1993). 'Government, NGOs and Agricultural Development: Perspectives on Changing Inter-Organisational Relationships.' *Journal of Development Studies* **29**(2): 199–219.

Bebbington, A. and Mitlin, D. (1996). 'NGO Capacity and Effectiveness: A Review of Themes in NGO-Related Research Recently Funded by ESCOR.' Unpublished report submitted to ESCOR.

Becker, E. (1998). 'Aid Groups are Hands that Help in Bosnia.' *New York Times* 12 April: 7.

Bennett, J. and Gibbs, S. (1996). *NGO Funding Strategies: An Introduction for Southern and Eastern NGOs*. Oxford: INTRAC.

Billis, D. and MacKeith, J. (1993). *Organising NGOs: Challenges and Trends in the Management of Overseas Aid*. London: Centre for Voluntary Organisations.

Brown, L.D. and Korten, D. (1991). 'Working More Effectively with Non Governmental Organizations.' Pp. 44–93 in Paul, S. and Israel, A. (eds) *Non Governmental Organizations and the World Bank*. Washington, DC: World Bank.

CARE (1994). Report of the Task Force on Partnership at CARE/USA. Unpublished mimeo.

Chazan, N. (1992). 'Africa's Democratic Challenge: Strengthening Civil Society and the State.' *World Policy Journal* **IX**(2): 279–307.

Clark, J. (1991). *Democratizing Development: The Role of Voluntary Organizations*. West Hartford, CT: Kumarian Press.

Commins, S. (1996). 'NGOs and the World Bank: Critical Engagement.' Discussion Papers Issue No. 3. Spring.

Conrad, W. and Glenn, W. (1983). *The Effective Voluntary Board of Directors*. London: Swallow Press.

Davies, R. (1996). 'Donor Information Demands and NGO Institutional Development.' Unpublished paper prepared for the 1996 Development Studies Association Conference, University of Reading (UK), 18–20 September.

Davis, D., Hulme, D., and Woodhouse, P. (1994). 'Decentralization by Default: Local Governance and the View from the Village in The Gambia.' *Public Administration and Development* **14**: 253–69.

Desai, V. (1995). *Filling the Gap: An Assessment of the Effectiveness of Urban NGOs*. ESCOR Research Report. London: Overseas Development Administration.

Fernandes, R.C. and Carneiro, L.P. (1995). 'Brazilian NGOs in the 1990s: A Survey.' In Reilly, C. (ed.) *New Paths to Democratic Development in Latin America: The Rise of NGO–Municipal Collaboration*. London: Lynne Reinner.

Fowler, A. (1988). 'Non-Governmental Organisations in Africa: Achieving Comparative Advantage in Relief and Micro-Development.' Discussion Paper 249. August. Institute of Development Studies.

Fox, J. (1996). 'How Does Civil Society Thicken? The Political Construction of Social Capital in Rural Mexico.' *World Development* **24**(6): 1089–103.

Gaer, F. (1995). 'Reality Check: Human Rights Nongovernmental Organisations Confront Governments at the United Nations.' *Third World Quarterly* **16**(3): 389–404.

GAFNA (1992). 'Gambia Food and Nutrition Association and Catholic Relief Services – USCC Fiscal Year 1993–1995 PL 480 Title II Multi-Year Operational Plan' (mimeo).

GARDA (1993). '1993 Review and Policy Framework.' GARDA.

Gaventa, J. (1995). 'Citizen Knowledge, Citizen Competence and Democracy Building.' *Good Society* **5**(3): 28–35.

Gopal, G. and Marc, A. (1994). *Study of Procurement and Disbursement Issues in Projects with Community Participation*. AFTHR Technical Note 17. April. Washington, DC: World Bank.

Heimovics, R., Herman, R., and Coughlin, J. (1993). 'Executive Leadership and Resource Dependence in Nonprofit Organizations: A Frame Analysis.' *Public Administration Review* **53**(5): 419–27.

Hellinger, D. (1989). 'An NGO Perspective on the World Bank.' *An NGO Guide to Trade and Finance in the Multilateral System*. New York: Non Governmental Liaison service: 31–5.

Hirschman, A. (1970). *Exit, Voice, and Loyalty: Responses to Decline in Firms, Organizations, and States*. Cambridge, MA: Harvard University Press.

James, R. (1994). *Strengthening the Capacity of Southern NGO Partners: A Survey of Current Northern NGO Approaches*. Oxford: INTRAC.

Keohane, R. and Nye, J. (1977). *Power and Interdependence: World Politics in Transition*. Boston, MA: Little.

Keohane, R. and Nye, J. (1989). *Power and Interdependence*. Second edition. HarperCollins.

Nelson, P. (1995). *The World Bank and NGOs: The Limits of Apolitical Development*. Basingstoke: Macmillan.

Opeskin, B. (1996). 'The Moral Foundations of Foreign Aid.' *World Development* **24**(1): 21–44.

Pearce, J. (1993). 'NGOs and Social Change: Agents or Facilitators?' *Development in Practice* **3**(3): 222–7.

Pfeffer, J. and Salancik, G. (1978). *The External Control of Organizations: A Resource Dependence Perspective*. New York: Harper and Row.

Reilly, C., ed. (1995).*New Paths to Democratic Development in Latin America: The Rise of NGO–Municipal Collaboration*. London: Lynne Reinner.

Renshaw, L.R. (1994). 'Strengthening Civil Society.'*Development* **4**: 46–9.

Rice, A. and Ritchie, C. (1995). 'Relationships between International Non-Governmental Organizations and the United Nations.'*Transnational Associations* **5**: 254–97.

Sallah, J. (1994). 'Community Resource Management Under the ANR Project: Lessons Learned from NRM in Africa.' Vol. 1 of 1. ANR Grants Administration, USAID/Banjuul Project No. 635-0236. December. Washington, DC: USAID.

Salmen, L. (1987). *Listen to the People*. Oxford: Oxford University Press.

Salmen, L. (1992). 'Reducing Poverty: An Institutional Perspective.' Washington, DC: World Bank.

Sollis, P. (1992). 'Multilateral Agencies, NGOs, and Policy Reform.' *Development in Practice* **2**(3): 163–78.

Tendler, J. (1982). 'Turning Private Voluntary Organizations into Development Agencies: Questions for Evaluation.' AID Program Evaluation Discussion Paper No. 12. April. Washington, DC: USAID.

Thompson, A. (1995). 'NGOs and Philanthropy in Latin America.' *Grassroots Development* **19**(2): 51–2.

Tomlinson, J. (1996). 'Building Sustainable Financing for Civil Society: Official Development Assistance and Foundation-Like Organisations in Southern Countries.' In Clayton, A. (ed.) *NGOs, Civil Society and the State: Building Democracy in Transitional Societies*. Oxford: INTRAC.

USAID (1995). 'Core Report of the New Partnerships Initiative.' Washington, DC: USAID. Unpublished draft version, 21 July.

USAID (1996). 'Endowments as a Tool for Sustainable Development.' USAID Working Paper No. 221. Washington, DC: Center for Development Information and Evaluation, USAID.

Wellard, K. and Copestake, J. (1993). *NGOs and the State in Africa: Rethinking Roles in Sustainable Agricultural Development*. London: Routledge.

Index